COLORED PEOPL

DATE DUE

~~AP 20 '99~~		
~~OC 19 '99~~		
~~MY 18 00~~		
~~JE 10 '00~~		
~~FE 6 01~~		
~~DE 17 04~~		

DEMCO 38-296

Colored People

ALSO BY HENRY LOUIS GATES, JR.

Loose Canons

Figures in Black

The Signifying Monkey

Colored People

A MEMOIR

Henry Louis Gates, Jr.

Alfred A. Knopf   NEW YORK   1994

THIS IS A BORZOI BOOK
PUBLISHED BY ALFRED A. KNOPF, INC.

A portion of this work was originally published in
The New Yorker.

Some of the names in this narrative have been changed.

Library of Congress Cataloging-in-Publication Data

Gates, Henry Louis.
Colored people / by Henry Louis Gates, Jr. — 1st ed.
p.   ;   cm.
ISBN 0-679-42179-3
1. Gates, Henry Louis—Childhood and youth.   2. Afro-
Americans—West Virginia—Social life and customs.   3. Afro-
American scholars—United States—Biography.   4. Critics—
United States—Biography.   I. Title.
PS29.G28A3   1993
975.4'00496073'092—dc20   93-12256
[B]   CIP

Manufactured in the United States of America

First Edition

I remember the very day when I became colored.

ZORA NEALE HURSTON

How dare anyone, parent, schoolteacher, or merely literary critic, tell me not to act colored?

ARNA BONTEMPS

For Henry Louis Gates, Sr.,
and in memory of
Pauline Augusta Coleman Gates

Contents

Preface

Dear Maggie and Liza:

I have written to you because a world into which I was born, a world that nurtured and sustained me, has mysteriously disappeared. My darkest fear is that Piedmont, West Virginia, will cease to exist, if some executives on Park Avenue decide that it is more profitable to build a completely new paper mill elsewhere than to overhaul one a century old. Then they would close it, just as they did in Cumberland with Celanese, and Pittsburgh Plate Glass, and the Kelly-Springfield Tire Company. The town will die, but our people will not move. They will not *be* moved. Because for them, Piedmont—snuggled between the Allegheny Mountains and the Potomac River Valley—is life itself.

I have written to you because of the day when we were driving home and you asked your mother and me just exactly what the civil rights movement had been all about and I pointed to a motel on Route 2 and said that at one time I could not have stayed there. Your mother could have stayed there, but your mother couldn't have stayed there with me. And you kids looked at us like we were telling you the biggest lie you had ever heard. So I thought about writing to you.

I have written for another reason, as well. I remember that once we were walking in Washington, D.C., heading for the National Zoo, and you asked me if I had known the man to whom I had just spoken. I said no. And, Liza, you volunteered that you found it embarrassing that I would speak to a complete stranger on the street. It called to mind a trip I'd made to Pittsburgh with my father. On the way from his friend Mr. Ozzie Washington's sister's house, I heard Daddy speak to a colored man, then saw him tip his hat to the man's wife. (Daddy liked nice hats: Caterpillar hats for work, Dobbs hats for Sunday.) It's just something that you do, he said, when I asked him if he had known those people and why had he spoken to them.

Last summer, I sat at a sidewalk café in Italy, and three or four "black" Italians walked casually by, as well as a dozen or more blacker Africans. Each spoke to me; rather, each nodded his head slightly or acknowledged me by a glance, ever so subtly. When I was growing up, we always did this with each other, passing boats in a sea of white folk.

Yet there were certain Negroes who would avoid acknowledging you in this way in an integrated setting, especially if the two of you were the ones doing the integrating. Don't go over there with those white people if all you're going to do is Jim Crow yourselves—Daddy must have said that to me a thousand times. And by that I think he meant we shouldn't *cling* to each other out of habit or fear, or use protective coloration to evade the risks of living like any other human being, or use clannishness as a cop-out for exploring ourselves and possibly making new selves, forged in the crucible of integration. Your black ass, he'd laugh, is integrated already.

But there are other reasons that people distrust the reflex—the nod, the glance, the murmured greeting.

One reason is a resentment at being lumped together with thirty million African Americans whom you don't know and

most of whom you will never know. Completely by the accident of racism, we have been bound together with people
with whom we may or may not have something in common,
just because we are "black." Thirty million Americans are
black, and thirty million is a lot of people. One day you wonder: What do the misdeeds of a Mike Tyson have to do with
me? So why do I feel implicated? And how can I not feel racial
recrimination when I can feel racial pride?

Then, too, there were Negroes who were embarrassed
about *being* Negroes, who didn't want to be bothered with
race and with other black people. One of the more painful
things about being colored was being colored in public around
other colored people, who were embarrassed to be colored
and embarrassed that we *both* were colored and in public
together. As if to say: "Negro, will you *pul-lease* disappear so
that I can get my own white people?" As if to say: "I'm not a
Negro like other Negroes." As if to say: "I am a human being—
let me be!"

For much of my adolescence and adulthood, I thought of
these people as having betrayed the race. I used to walk up
to them and call them *Brother* or *Sister*, loud and with a
sardonic edge, when they looked like they were trying to
"escape." When I went off to college, I would make the "con-
version" of errant classmates a serious project, a political commitment.

I used to reserve my special scorn for those Negroes who
were always being embarrassed by someone else in the
race. Someone too dark, someone too "loud," someone too
"wrong." Someone who dared to wear red in public. Loud
and wrong: we used to say that about each other. Nigger is
loud and wrong. "Loud" carried a triple meaning: speaking
too loudly, dressing too loudly, and just *being* too loudly.

I do know that, when I was a boy, many Negroes would
have been the first to censure other Negroes once they were

admitted into all-white neighborhoods or schools or clubs. "An embarrassment to the race"—phrases of that sort were bandied about. Accordingly, many of us in our generation engaged in strange antics to flout those strictures. Like eating watermelon in public, eating it loudly and merrily, and spitting the seeds into the middle of the street, red juice running down the sides of our cheeks, collecting under our chins. Or taking the greatest pride in the Royal Kink. Uncle Harry used to say he didn't *like* watermelon, which I knew was a lie because I saw him wolf down slices when I was a little kid, before he went off to seminary at Boston University. But he came around, just like he came around to painting God and Jesus black, and all the seraphim and the cherubim, too. And I, from another direction, have gradually come around, also, and stopped trying to tell other Negroes how to be black.

Do you remember when your mother and I woke you up early on a Sunday morning, just to watch Nelson Mandela walk out of prison, and how it took a couple of hours for him to emerge, and how you both wanted to go back to bed and, then, to watch cartoons? And how we began to worry that something bad had happened to him on the way out, because the delay was so long? And when he finally walked out of that prison, how we were so excited and teary-eyed at Mandela's nobility, his princeliness, his straight back and unbowed head? I think I felt that there walked the Negro, as Pop might have said; there walked the whole of the African people, as regal as any king. And that feeling I had, that gooseflesh sense of identity that I felt at seeing Nelson Mandela, listening to Mahalia Jackson sing, watching Muhammad Ali fight, or hearing Martin Luther King speak, is part of what I mean by being colored. I realize the sentiment may not be logical, but I want to have my cake and eat it, too. Which is why I still nod or speak to black people on the streets and why it felt so good to be acknowledged by the Afro-Italians who passed my table at the café in Milan.

I want to be able to take special pride in a Jessye Norman aria, a Muhammad Ali shuffle, a Michael Jordan slam dunk, a Spike Lee movie, a Thurgood Marshall opinion, a Toni Morrison novel, James Brown's Camel Walk. Above all, I enjoy the unselfconscious moments of a shared cultural intimacy, whatever form they take, when no one else is watching, when no white people are around. Like Joe Louis's fights, which my father still talks about as part of the fixed repertoire of stories that texture our lives. You've seen his eyes shining as he describes how Louis hit Max Schmeling so many times and so hard, and how some reporter asked him, after the fight: "Joe, what would you have done if that last punch hadn't knocked Schmeling out?" And how ole Joe responded, without missing a beat: "I'da run around behind him to see what was holdin' him up!"

Even so, I rebel at the notion that I can't be part of other groups, that I can't construct identities through elective affinity, that race must be the most important thing about me. Is that what I want on my gravestone: Here lies an African American? So I'm divided. I want to be black, to know black, to luxuriate in whatever I might be calling blackness at any particular time—but to do so in order to come out the other side, to experience a humanity that is neither colorless nor reducible to color. Bach *and* James Brown. Sushi *and* fried catfish. Part of me admires those people who can say with a straight face that they have transcended any attachment to a particular community or group . . . but I always want to run around behind them to see what holds them up.

I am not Everynegro. I am not native to the great black metropolises: New York, Chicago, or Los Angeles, say. Nor can I claim to be a "citizen of the world." I am from and of a time and a place—Piedmont, West Virginia—and that's a world apart, a world of difference. So this is not a story of a race but a story of a village, a family, and its friends. And of a sort of segregated peace. What hurt me most about the glorious black awakening of the late sixties and early seventies is that we lost our sense of humor. Many of us thought that enlightened politics excluded it.

In your lifetimes, I suspect, you will go from being African Americans, to "people of color," to being, once again, "colored people." (The linguistic trend toward condensation is strong.) I don't mind any of the names myself. But I have to confess that I like "colored" best, maybe because when I hear the word, I hear it in my mother's voice and in the sepia tones of my childhood. As artlessly and honestly as I can, I have tried to evoke a colored world of the fifties, a Negro world of the early sixties, and the advent of a black world of the later sixties, from the point of view of the boy I was. When you are old enough to read what follows, I hope that it brings you even a small measure of understanding, at long last, of why we see the world with such different eyes . . . and why that is for me a source both of gladness and of regret. And I hope you'll understand why I continue to speak to colored people I pass on the streets.

Love,
Daddy

Piedmont, West Virginia
July 8, 1993

I / Will the Circle Be Unbroken?

1 / Colored People

On the side of a hill in the Allegheny Mountains, two and a half hours northwest of Washington and southeast of Pittsburgh, slathered along the ridge of "Old Baldie" mountain like butter on the jagged side of a Parker House roll, sits Piedmont, West Virginia (population 2,565 in 1950, when I was born), the second major city of Mineral County. West Virginia is famous for its hills, the Allegheny Mountains, which run along the Potomac River in the east, the Ohio along the west, and the Kanawha and Guyandotte in the south. And of all the mountain ranges gazed upon by its riverine mountaineers, none is more beautiful than the south branch of the Potomac Valley, overlooked by Gates Point, the highest promontory in the county, rising above Patterson's Creek.

It was in Piedmont that most of the colored people of Mineral County lived—351 out a total population of 22,000.

You wouldn't know Piedmont anymore—my Piedmont, I mean—by its silhouetted ruins. Not the town that stands there now with its dignity assaulted by the consolidation of the Mineral County school system, and its sense of itself

3

humbled by the abolition of its high school basketball team. "Daddy, that school is *dead*," Liza once said—she couldn't have been more than four—when she saw what once had been my elementary school. Even then she had a lot of mouth— such an evil, threatening quality to have around the Coleman family that I cultivated it all my childhood, as best I could. How else was I going to keep at bay the hovering, censorious presence of my uncles, Mama's nine brothers?

Liza was right, though: the Davis Free School, Piedmont's sole elementary school, founded in 1906 and once a proud three-story red-brick building perched high on top of Kenny House Hill, is now, quite visibly, dead. If it is not yet buried, its rotting corpse is being plucked apart by masonry buzzards feeding off its finely crafted crimson bricks.

To my children, Piedmont as a whole must seem to be a graying, desiccated town, rotting away brick by brick, just like my old school. Its population is down to about eleven hundred souls, three hundred of whom are black, a population whose average age increases each year, so that the spirited figures who dominated my youth—those who survive, anyway— must strike my daughters as grizzled elders. No, my children will never know Piedmont, never experience the magic I can still feel in the place where I learned how to be a colored boy.

The fifties in Piedmont was a sepia time, or at least that's the color my memory has given it. Piedmont was prosperous and growing, a village of undoubted splendors. I say a village, but that's an unpopular usage among some. ("Class Three City" is the official West Virginia state euphemism.) My cousin Greg, for example, complained when I called it that in a magazine article I wrote. "Hey, boy," he had begun, familiarly enough. (We call each other "boy.") "You got to explain something to me. How you going to call Piedmont a *village*?"

Village or town, or something in between—no matter. Peo-

ple from Piedmont were always proud to be from Piedmont—
nestled against a wall of mountains, smack-dab on the banks
of the mighty Potomac. We knew God gave America no more
beautiful location.

And its social topography was something we knew like the
back of our hands. Piedmont was an immigrant town. White
Piedmont was Italian and Irish, with a handful of wealthy
WASPs on East Hampshire Street, and "ethnic" neighborhoods of working-class people everywhere else, colored and
white. Start with the elementary school, or what was left of it
that day when Liza pronounced it dead. If you go west, up
the hill toward the colored VFW (where Pop goes every day
at four in the afternoon to see his old buddies and drink water
glasses of gin and orange juice on crushed ice for seventy-five
cents), you'll see one of the two Italian neighborhoods, home
to the Barbaritos, the DiPilatos, the DiBualdos, and a whole
lot of other people whose names end in *o*. (The new colored
VFW was the old Knights of Columbus when I was a kid.) A
street above the Italians lived the Irish: the O'Rourkes, the
O'Briens, the O'Reillys, the O'Neills, and a whole lot of other
people whose names begin with *o*. At one time, two of my
best friends were Finnegan Lannon and Johnny DiPilato.

Now, the whole west side of Piedmont, "Up on the Hill,"
as the people "Downtown" still say, was called "Arch Hill." I
figured that it was called that because it was shaped like the
arch of your foot. Twenty-five years later, I learned that what
the colored people called "Arch Hill" had all along been "Irish
Hill." Cracked me up when Pop told me that. "Dummy," was
all he said.

For as long as anybody can remember, Piedmont's character has always been completely bound up with the West-
vaco paper mill: its prosperous past and its doubtful future.
At first glance, Piedmont is a typical dying mill town, with
the crumbling infrastructure and the resignation of its peo-

ple to its gentle decline. Many once beautiful buildings have been abandoned. They stand empty and unkempt, and testify to a bygone time of spirit and pride. The big houses on East Hampshire Street are no longer proud, but they were when I was a kid.

On still days, when the air is heavy, Piedmont has the rotten-egg smell of a chemistry class. The acrid, sulfurous odor of the bleaches used in the paper mill drifts along the valley, penetrating walls and clothing, furnishings and skin. No perfume can fully mask it. It is as much a part of the valley as is the river, and the people who live there are not overly disturbed by it. "Smells like money to me," we were taught to say in its defense, even as children.

The rich white people lived on upper East Hampshire Street—the Hudsons (insurance, Coca-Cola stock) in their big white Federal home, the Campbells (coal, insurance, real estate) in a gingerbread Victorian, the Drains (a judge) in their square brick, and the Arnolds (insurance) in a curving Queen Anne. You can tell from the East Hampshire Street architecture that wealthy people with fine architects took great pains to wear their wealth in their houses and, as Jean Toomer says in *Cane* of his character Rhobert, wear their houses on their heads. Mr. Campbell, whose family was once listed as among the richest in the country, built himself a veritable Victorian castle. Even when I was a little boy, walking past that house with my father in the evenings after work, I'd dream about owning it. Penny Baker, whose father was the mayor, Jeff Baker, later told me that was her fantasy too. So I suppose that most of the children in Piedmont dreamed that same dream.

Just below East Hampshire, as if a diagonal had been drawn from it downward at a thirty-degree angle, was Pearl Street, which the colored people called "Rat Tail Road," because it snaked down around the hill to the bottom of the valley, where the tracks of the B & O run on their way to Keyser, the county seat. Poor white people like Bonnie Gilroy's family lived down there, and five black families. We moved there when I was four. White people also lived "over in the Orchard," near the high school and the swimming pool.

Colored people lived in three neighborhoods: "Downtown," on Back Street, which we called "Black Street"—but only when our parents weren't around, since "black" was not a word for polite company back then; "Up on the Hill," or on Erin Street, just one street above East Hampshire; and down Rat Tail Road. Colored people, in fact, occupied the highest street in town, and the house where Mama's mother, Big Mom, lived occupied the highest point Up on the Hill. Like the Italians and the Irish, most of the colored people migrated to Piedmont at the turn of the century to work at the paper mill, which opened in 1888.

Nearly everybody in the Tri-Towns worked there. The Tri-Towns—three towns of similar size—were connected by two bridges across sections of the Potomac less than a mile apart: Piedmont, West Virginia; Luke, Maryland; and Westernport, Maryland, the westernmost navigable point on the river, between Pittsburgh and the Chesapeake Bay. The Italians and the Irish of Arch Hill, along with a few of the poorer white people, worked the good jobs in the paper mill, including all those in the craft unions. That mattered, because crafts demanded skill and training, and craftsmen commanded high wages. It was not until 1968 that the craft unions at the mill were integrated.

Until the summer of 1968, all the colored men at the paper mill worked on "the platform"—loading paper into trucks. "The loaders," they were called, because that's what they did. (When we were being evil, we called them "the loafers.") The end product of the paper mill was packaged in skids, big wooden crates of paper, which could weigh as much as seven thousand pounds each. The skids had to be forklifted from the mill onto the shipping platform and then loaded into the huge tractor-trailers that took them to Elsewhere. Loading is what Daddy did every working day of his working life. That's what almost every colored grown-up I knew did. Every day at 6:30 a.m., Daddy would go off to the mill, and he'd work until 3:30 p.m., when the mill whistle would blow. So important was the mill to the life of the town that school let out at the same time. We would eat dinner at 4:00, so that Pop could get to his second job, as a janitor at the telephone company, by 4:30. His workday ended at 7:30, except when there was a baseball game, over in the Orchard or at the park in Westernport, in which case he would cut out early.

Almost all the colored people in Piedmont worked at the paper mill and made the same money, because they all worked at the same job, on the platform. I said almost all: Some colored worked for the B & O, and some at Celanese or Kelly-Springfield, both of which had their start right down to Cumberland. A few men did service jobs, like Mr. Shug, the blackest man in Piedmont, who was ole Miss Campbell's driver and who, people would laugh, did most of his best driving at night. Shug lived with Miss Fanchion, and though they weren't married, nobody seemed to mind.

But of course, the colored world was not so much a neighborhood as a condition of existence. And though our own world was seemingly self-contained, it impinged upon the white world of Piedmont in almost every direction. Certainly, the borders of our world seemed to be encroached upon when some white man or woman would show up where he or she did not belong.

Like when some white man would show up at the Legion, cruising "to get laid by a colored woman," or some jug-headed loader would bring his white buddy to a party or a dance and then beg some woman to "give him some." Sometimes the loader pandered for money, sometimes for a favor at the mill, sometimes for nothing in particular, just a vague desire for approval.

On other occasions, it might be some hungry white woman, hair peroxide blond and teased up, neckline plunging, and pants too tight, sitting at the bar as if she were the Queen of England, ennobled by untrammeled desire: feasting on the desire for the forbidden in the colored men's eyes, while they in turn feasted on the desire in hers. You could always tell when a white woman was in the bar: they played slow music all night long.

Our space was violated when one of *them* showed up. The rhythms would be off. The music would sound not quite right: attempts to pat the beat off just so. Everybody would leave early. People would say they'd had a good time but they were tired for some reason, or had to get up early to go to work. Or else they'd get ugly, and somebody would slap somebody else, usually his own wife.

When Daddy was a teenager, dance bands used to come to the Crystal Palace Ballroom in Cumberland. They'd play a set or two in the evening for white people and then a special midnight show for the colored. Daddy says *everybody* would be there—the maimed, the sick, the dying, and the dead. Duke Ellington. Cab Calloway. And Piedmont's own Don Redman. Later, we had our own places to dance—the colored American Legion, and then the VFW.

It was amazing to me how new dances would spread in the black community, even to small towns like ours. Somebody'd be visiting his relatives somewhere, go to a party, and that would be that. He'd bring it back and teach everyone, showing it off in the streets in the evenings or at a party in somebody's basement. Darnell Allen and Richard Bruce, Sheila Washington and Gloria Jean Taylor were the best dancers in the town. They could learn *any* dance in a few minutes, and they'd take the floor, improvising and modifying as they went along. By the evening's end, the dance was *theirs*. They'd own it, having by then invented the Piedmont version. Then it became *ours*. Sometimes they'd just watch it on TV, like on the Dick Clark or Milt Grant shows. Much later, they'd watch *Soul Train*. Gloria Jean could dance just like James Brown; so could Audie Galloway.

Inez Jones was Queen of the Dance, though. When she danced the Dirty Dog with Jimmy Adamson, everybody would stop to stare. Like watching two dogs in heat for what seemed like hours. Then she'd take Jimmy's handkerchief out of his back pocket and rub it between her legs, like she was buffing a leather shoe. The crowd would go crazy. Meltdown. Somebody would put on James Brown's version of "Lost Someone," which plays for nine minutes, on that *Live at the Apollo* album, and everybody would grab somebody and start to grind. "Call me Coffee," the guys would say, "cuz I grind so fine." That's when the fights would start, if somebody's woman or man seemed to be percolating too much coffee with the wrong person. Usually it was a matter of fisticuffs, and every major holiday, there was a fight. Sometimes knives would come into play. People go crazy over sex, Daddy would warn me, even before I knew what sex was.

Things could get ugly, ugly and dark—like the way Bobby Lee Jones, a classmate of my brother Rocky's, looked that day he beat his woman, his tacky red processed strands dangling down the middle of his forehead, his Johnson getting harder each time he slapped her face. They say he would have fucked her right then and there if he hadn't been so drunk that his arms got tired of swinging at her, her with her face smeared with blue-black eye shadow, miserable and humiliated. Or the time some guy cut off the tip of Russell Jones's nose after he had grabbed him for feeling up Inez, Inez's thighs smoking from doing the dog, her handkerchief wet from her rubbing it between her legs, men fighting for the right to sniff that rag like it was the holy grail. Don't no man know that love, Mr. Chile Green would say when somebody would play the dozens about how ugly his girlfriend's face was.

Yeah, I missed going to those dances, though I didn't miss Inez Jones: I was too young then. And then Darnell and Sheila and Richard Bruce joined the Holiness Church, soon after I got religion myself, so all I was missing them do was the Holy Dance, right across the street from our church. I said to Richard I was sorry he couldn't dance anymore. He told me he was dancing for the Lord. His father—the one whose wife Roebuck Johnson was making love to every afternoon after work—was hard on him too. Said Richard wasn't *his*. The Lord provideth, Richard would say. His ways are inscrutable.

Before 1955, most white people were only shadowy presences in our world, vague figures of power like remote bosses at the mill or tellers at the bank. There were exceptions, of course, the white people who would come into our world in ritualized, everyday ways we all understood. Mr. Mail Man, Mr. Insurance Man, Mr. White-and-Chocolate Milk Man, Mr. Landlord Man, Mr. Po-lice Man: we called white people by their trade, like allegorical characters in a mystery play. Mr. Insurance Man would come by every other week to collect premiums on college or death policies, sometimes fifty cents or less. But my favorite white visitor was the Jewel Tea Man, who arrived in his dark-brown helmet-shaped truck, a sort of modified jeep, and, like the Sears Man, brought new appliances to our house. I loved looking at his catalogues. Mr. Jewel Tea Man, may I see your catalogues? Please?

Or they were doctors. Mine was Young Doc Wolverton. We dressed up when we went to see the doctor. That made sense to me because I wanted to be a doctor; Mama wanted both of her sons to be doctors. Young Doc Wolverton owned our house, or at least the house we moved to when I was four. And that was another thing: As much as we belonged to Piedmont, as much as Piedmont belonged to us, colored weren't allowed to own property, not until the 1970s, anyway. All our houses were rented from white landowners, and that was just the way it was. It drove my mother crazy.

Before we lived in the house rented from Doc Wolverton, we lived in a much smaller house, at the base of Big Mom's hill, or at the top of Fredlock Street before the blacktop ran out and Big Mom's gravel driveway started. My sense of that house comes more from Mama's recollections of it than from my own. Some of her memories feel like my own, like the day in 1951 when Bobby Thomson hit a home run in the bottom of the ninth to beat the Dodgers and win the pennant for the Giants, and my father went absolutely crazy and began to hop from chair to table to sofa to chair, round and round the perimeter of our living room. It scared me so much that I started to cry.

And of course, we would bump into the white world at the hospital in Keyser or at the credit union in Westernport or in one of the stores downtown. But our neighborhoods were clearly demarcated, as if by ropes or turnstiles. Welcome to the Colored Zone, a large stretched banner could have said. And it felt good in there, like walking around your house in bare feet and underwear, or snoring right out loud on the couch in front of the TV—swaddled by the comforts of home, the warmth of those you love.

Even when we went Downtown, our boundaries were pre-scribed: we'd congregate on the steps of the First National Bank of Piedmont, chewing up the world, analyzing the world as it walked or drove by, court in session, James Helms presiding in his porkpie hat. Helms was one of Daddy's coworkers, the one who talked the most. When he was drunk. Which, as near as I could see, was almost all the time.

White man *knows* not to fuck with us, Helms would opine judicially. We treat them good around here.

And nobody in their right mind likes skinny legs, either, someone would volunteer, if the subject needed shifting. Nothing worse than a woman with no butt and legs as skinny as pencils. Like the Lennon sisters on *Lawrence Welk*, which Daddy watched for the big band sound, reminding him of the old Crystal Palace in Cumberland, when Duke Ellington's or Cab Calloway's band would come to town. Or like Diana Ross, whose shapely legs were widely bemoaned as too thin. I'd rather have no titties than no butt, but I'm a thigh man myself, James Helms would avow.

I never knew what the women said about the men, but I know they said a lot. I was always disappointed when the women, talking and laughing in the kitchen, would stop when I came within earshot and shift to safer subjects—or begin to spell out words they had been speaking freely and with so much pleasure just a few minutes before. (That stopped the day I spelled one of those words back to my mother and asked what it meant. From the horrified look on her face, I knew it had to be a bad one.)

Another major preoccupation of the people's court, naturally, was the sins, venal and venial, of kith and kin. People at home would customarily say that the woman was "running" the man. It was always the woman's fault. And she was always bad. Not bad for loving, but bad for embarrassing her husband or her parents in the Valley with No Secrets. You couldn't get away with anything in Piedmont. Most people just did it as discreetly as they could, knowing not only that everybody colored knew but also that their name would be in the streets every day, permanently and forever, whenever the conversation lagged, new business being over, and old business was called up to pass the time. The biggest gossips were the loaders, who talked trash and talked shit all day long. The loaders

were the Colored Genealogical Society, keepers of genetic
impurities. The loaders were the Senate, the House, and the
Supreme Court of Public Opinion, cross-fertilizing culture,
gossip, and sometimes each other's wives.

Few women lived alone, without husbands. Those who did
worked as maids or cleaning ladies; and they were poor. And
there were a few town drunks, like Mr. Tyler Simon, who I
don't think I ever saw sober. Unlike the hard-drinking James
Helms, Mr. Tyler couldn't hold a job. He was always trying
to get on at the mill, always failing, always poor, always drunk.
His daughter, Marilyn, was the first black valedictorian at
the high school, in 1967. Marilyn was shy, very quiet, and
sensitive. You could tell that she didn't feel pretty, the way
she held her head down all the time. She wore drab colors
too. Plain blues and browns. Her clothes looked homemade,
or secondhand.

Marilyn had gone to the university at Morgantown right
away, without going to Potomac State, in Keyser, first, like
everybody else. Nobody blamed her, somehow, though they
would have blamed someone else, because skipping Potomac
State was like betraying your family by leaving home too early.
Ain't no need to be away from Piedmont for more than two
years; three years max. Even the army keeps you only three
years. The only exemption was if you were to make it into
baseball's major leagues. Then it would be okay. Play in the
big leagues till you're too old, then come on home. Besides,
there's always the off-season, and you can come back then,
hunting and fishing with everyone else, just like the old days,
washing the dust out of your system at the VFW at four
o'clock. People in Piedmont were never crazy about change,
which is one reason they always voted against putting fluoride
in the water and consolidating the high schools in Mineral
County.

One day, in Marilyn's freshman year, this guy came to

Morgantown on a motorcycle, and whatever rap he had must have been heavy-duty, because she just climbed onto the back of his motorcycle and drove away. Just like that. Didn't even pack her bags or take her books. Never to be seen again. Guess Marilyn always wanted to fly away. That's how the colored people tell it.

Her daddy drank, it was said, because Mr. Johnson was running her mother, and after Tyler, Jr., was born, the babies started getting darker and having heads shaped like Mr. Johnson's. Her mother had a sister and they were both pretty. I used to imagine them dressed up in yellow polka-dotted dresses with bows in their hair, singing "Double your pleasure, double your fun, with Doublemint, Doublemint, Doublemint gum," like those white girls on the TV commercials, and making lots of money, so maybe Mr. Tyler would stop drinking. Mr. Johnson made love to the sister too. *Her* husband, Ray Sanders, drank on top of diabetes and would fry up ham and bacon and sausage for breakfast, directly defying his doctor's orders. That high blood pressure stuff, he'd say, that only applies to white people. We *used* to this stuff. They removed his second leg just after he went blind.

Eating and drinking yourself to death in front of the TV, aggravating heart disease and "high blood," the way Tyler and Ray did, was a substitute for violence that people could understand, rage turned inward. What was puzzling was when someone such as Marilyn suddenly followed an aberrant flight pattern, like an addled bird that has mistaken or forsaken its species.

People in Piedmont were virulent nationalists—Piedmont nationalists. And this was our credo:

All New York's got that Piedmont's got is more of what we got. Same, but bigger. And, if you were a student: *You can get a good education* anywhere. *They got the same books, ain't they? Just bigger classes, 'at's all.*

Otherwise the advantage was all to Piedmont. Did you know that Kenny House Hill was written about in "Ripley's Believe It or Not" as the only street in the world from which you can enter all three stories of the same building? That made it the most famous place in this Class Three City; other of our attractions were less well publicized.

Like Dent Davis's bologna, which was so good that when colored people came home to Piedmont for the mill picnic each Labor Day, they would take pounds of it back to whatever sorry homes they had forsaken Piedmont for, along with bright-red cans of King Syrup (a concoction that the colored people called King-ro, as a conflation of King and Karo), with the inset metal circle for a lid, the kind that you had to pry open with the back of a claw hammer, and what looked like the MGM lion centered on its front label. Some of them, those whose tastes were most rarefied, would take home a few jars of our tap water. And that was before anybody thought of *buying* water in bottles. People in Piedmont can't imagine that today. A dollar for a bottle of *water*! We had some *good* water in Piedmont, the best drinking water in the world, if you asked any of us.

Dent's bologna, and our water, and our King Syrup, and the paper mill's annual pic-a-nic, all helped account for Piedmont's tenacious grip upon its inhabitants, even those in diaspora. And then there was our Valley. I never knew colored people anywhere who were crazier about mountains and water, flowers and trees, fishing and hunting. For as long as anyone could remember, we could outhunt, outshoot, and outswim the white boys in the Valley. We didn't flaunt our rifles and shotguns, though, because that might make the white people too nervous. Pickup trucks and country music— now that was going *too* far, at least in the fifties. But that would come, too, over time, once integration had hit the second generation. The price of progress, I guess.

2 / Prime Time

I guess some chafed more than others against the mundane impediments of the color line. "It's no disgrace to be colored," the black entertainer Bert Williams famously observed early in this century, "but it is awfully inconvenient." For most of my childhood, we couldn't eat in restaurants or sleep in hotels, we couldn't use certain bathrooms or try on clothes in stores. Mama insisted that we dress up when we went to shop. She was a fashion plate when she went to clothing stores, and wore white pads called shields under her arms so her dress or blouse would show no sweat. We'd like to try this on, she'd say carefully, articulating her words precisely and properly. We don't buy clothes we can't try on, she'd say when they declined, as we'd walk, in Mama's dignified manner, out of the store. She preferred to shop where we had an account and where everyone knew who she was.

As for me, I hated the fact that we couldn't sit down in the Cut-Rate. No one colored was allowed to, with one exception: my father. It was as if there were a permanent TAKE-AWAY ONLY sign for colored people. You were supposed to stand at the counter, get your food to go, and leave. I don't know for certain why Carl Dadisman, the proprietor, wouldn't stop Daddy from sitting down. But I believe it was in part because Daddy was so light-complected, and in part because, during his shift at the phone company, he picked up orders for food and coffee for the operators, and Dadisman relied on that business. At the time, I never wondered if it occurred to Daddy not to sit down at the Cut-Rate when neither his wife nor his two children were allowed to, although now that I am a parent myself, the strangeness of it crosses my mind on occasion.

Even when we were with Daddy, you see, we had to stand at the counter and order takeout, then eat on white paper plates using plastic spoons, sipping our vanilla rickeys from green-and-white paper cups through plastic flexible-end straws. Even after basketball games, when Young Doc Bess would set up the team with free Cokes after one of the team's many victories, the colored players had to stand around and drink out of paper cups while the white players and cheerleaders sat down in the red Naugahyde booths and drank out of glasses. Integrate? I'll shut it down first, Carl Dadisman had vowed. He was an odd-looking man, with a Humpty-Dumpty sort of head and bottom, and weighing four or five hundred pounds. He ran the taxi service, too, and was just as nice as he could be, even to colored people. But he did not want us sitting in his booths, eating off his plates and silverware, putting our thick greasy lips all over his glasses. He'd retire first, or die.

He had a heart attack one day while sitting in the tiny toilet at his place of business. Daddy and some other men tried to lift him up, while he was screaming and gasping and clutching his chest, but he was stuck in that cramped space. They called the rescue squad at the Fire Department. Lowell Taylor and Pat Amoroso came. Lowell was black and was the star of the soccer team at the high school across the river in Westernport. He looked like Pele, down to the shape of his head.

They sawed and sawed and sawed, while the ambulance and the rescue squad sat outside on Third Street, blocking the driveway to the town's parking lot. After a while, Carl Dadisman's cries and moans became quieter and quieter. Finally, they wedged in a couple of two-by-fours and dragged out his lifeless body. By then it made little difference to Carl that Lowell was black.

Maybe Carl never understood that the racial dispensation he took for granted was coming to an end. As a child, I must once have assumed that this dispensation could no more be contested than the laws of gravity, or traffic lights. And I'm not sure when I realized otherwise.

I know that I had rich acquaintance early on with the inconveniences to which Bert Williams alluded. But segregation had some advantages, like the picnic lunch Mama would make for the five-hour train ride on the National Limited to Parkersburg, where you had to catch the bus down to the state capital, Charleston, to visit her sister Loretta. So what if we didn't feel comfortable eating in the dining car? Our food was better. Fried chicken, baked beans, and potato salad . . . a book and two decks of cards . . . and I didn't care if the train ever got there. We'd sing or read in our own section, munching that food and feeling sorry for the people who couldn't get any, and play 500 or Tonk or Fish with Mama and Daddy, until we fell asleep.

The simple truth is that the civil rights era came late to Piedmont, even though it came early to our television set. We could watch what was going on Elsewhere on television, but the marches and sit-ins were as remote to us as, in other ways, was the all-colored world of *Amos and Andy*—a world full of black lawyers, black judges, black nurses, black doctors.

Politics aside, though, we were starved for images of ourselves and searched TV to find them. Everybody, of course, watched sports, because Piedmont was a big sports town. Making the big leagues was like getting to Heaven, and everybody had hopes that they could, or a relative could. We'd watch the games day and night, and listen on radio to what we couldn't see. Everybody knew the latest scores, batting averages, rbi's, and stolen bases. Everybody knew the standings in the leagues, who could still win the pennant and how. Everybody liked the Dodgers because of Jackie Robinson, the same way everybody still voted Republican because of Abraham Lincoln. Sports on the mind, sports in the mind. The only thing to rival the Valley in fascination was the big-league baseball diamond.

I once heard Mr. James Helms say, "You got to give the white man his due when it comes to technology. One on one, though, and it's even-steven. Joe Louis showed 'em that." We were obsessed with sports in part because it was the only time we could compete with white people even-steven. And the white people, it often seemed, were just as obsessed with this primal confrontation between the races as we were. I think they integrated professional sports, after all those years of segregation, just to capitalize on this voyeuristic thrill of the forbidden contact. What interracial sex was to the seventies, interracial sports were to the fifties. Except for sports, we rarely saw a colored person on TV.

Actually, I first got to know white people as "people" through their flickering images on television shows. It was the television set that brought us together at night, and the television set that brought in the world outside the Valley. We were close enough to Washington to receive its twelve channels on cable. Piedmont was transformed from a radio culture to one with the fullest range of television, literally overnight. During my first-grade year, we'd watch *Superman*, *Lassie*, Jack Benny, Danny Thomas, *Robin Hood*, *I Love Lucy*, *December Bride*, Nat King Cole (of course), *Wyatt Earp*, *Broken Arrow*, Phil Silvers, Red Skelton, *The $64,000 Question*, *Ozzie and Harriet*, *The Millionaire*, *Father Knows Best*,

The Lone Ranger, Bob Cummings, *Dragnet, The People's Choice, Rin Tin Tin, Jim Bowie, Gunsmoke, My Friend Flicka, The Life of Riley, Topper, Dick Powell's Zane Grey Theater, Circus Boy,* and Loretta Young—all in prime time. My favorites were *The Life of Riley,* in part because he worked in a factory like Daddy did, and *Ozzie and Harriet,* in part because Ozzie never seemed to work at all. A year later, however, *Leave It to Beaver* swept most of the others away.

With a show like *Topper,* I felt as if I was getting a glimpse, at last, of the life that Mrs. Hudson, and Mrs. Thomas, and Mrs. Campbell, must be leading in their big mansions on East Hampshire Street. Smoking jackets and cravats, spats and canes, elegant garden parties and martinis. People who wore suits to eat dinner! This was a world so elegantly distant from ours, it was like a voyage to another galaxy, light-years away.

Leave It to Beaver, on the other hand, was a world much closer, but just out of reach nonetheless. Beaver's street was where we wanted to live, Beaver's house where we wanted to eat and sleep, Beaver's father's firm where we'd have liked Daddy to work. These shows for us were about property, the property that white people could own and that we couldn't. About a level of comfort and ease at which we could only wonder. It was the world that the integrated school was going to prepare us to enter and that, for Mama, would be the prize.

If prime time consisted of images of middle-class white people who looked nothing at all like us, late night was about the radio, listening to *Randy's Record Shop* from Gallatin, Tennessee. My brother, Rocky, kept a transistor radio by his bed, and he'd listen to it all night, for all I knew, long after I'd fallen asleep. In 1956, black music hadn't yet broken down into its many subgenres, except for large divisions such as jazz, blues, gospel, rhythm and blues. On *Randy's,* you were as likely to hear The Platters doing "The Great Pretender" and Clyde McPhatter doing "Treasure of Love" as you were to hear Howlin' Wolf do "Smokestack Lightning" or Joe Turner do "Corrine, Corrine." My own favorite that year was the slow, deliberate sound of Jesse Belvin's "Goodnight, My Love." I used to fall asleep singing it in my mind to my Uncle Earkie's girlfriend, Ula, who was a sweet caffè latté brown, with the blackest, shiniest straight hair and the fullest, most rounded red lips. Not even in your dreams, he had said to me one day, as I watched her red dress slink down our front stairs. It was my first brush with the sublime.

We used to laugh at the way the disc jockey sang "Black Strap Lax-a-teeves" during the commercials. I sometimes would wonder if the kids we'd seen on TV in Little Rock or Birmingham earlier in the evening were singing themselves to sleep with *their* Ulas.

Lord knows, we weren't going to learn how to be colored by watching television. Seeing somebody colored on TV was an event.

"Colored, colored, on Channel Two," you'd hear someone shout. Somebody else would run to the phone, while yet another hit the front porch, telling all the neighbors where to see it. And *everybody* loved *Amos and Andy*—I don't care what people say today. For the colored people, the day they took *Amos and Andy* off the air was one of the saddest days in Piedmont, about as sad as the day of the last mill pic-a-nic.

What was special to us about *Amos and Andy* was that their world was *all* colored, just like ours. Of course, *they* had their colored judges and lawyers and doctors and nurses, which we could only dream about having, or becoming—and we *did* dream about those things. Kingfish ate his soft-boiled eggs delicately, out of an egg cup. He even owned an acre of land in Westchester County, which he sold to Andy, using the facade of a movie set to fake a mansion. As far as we were concerned, the foibles of Kingfish or Calhoun the lawyer were the foibles of individuals who happened to be funny. Nobody was likely to confuse them with the colored people we knew, no more than we'd confuse ourselves with the entertainers and athletes we saw on TV or in *Ebony* or *Jet*, the magazines we devoured to keep up with what was happening with the race. And people took special relish in Kingfish's malapropisms. "I denies the allegation, Your Honor, and I resents the alligator."

In one of my favorite episodes of *Amos and Andy*, "The Punjab of Java-Pour," Andy Brown is hired to advertise a brand of coffee and is required to dress up as a turbaned Oriental potentate. Kingfish gets the bright idea that if he dresses up as a potentate's servant, the two of them can enjoy a vacation at a luxury hotel for free. So attired, the two promenade around the lobby, running up an enormous tab and generously dispensing "rubies" and "diamonds" as tips. The plan goes awry when people try to redeem the gems and discover them to be colored glass. It was widely suspected that this episode was what prompted two Negroes in Baltimore to dress like African princes and demand service in a segregated four-star restaurant. Once it was clear to the management that these were not American Negroes, the two were treated royally. When the two left the restaurant, they took off their African headdresses and robes and enjoyed a hearty laugh at the restaurant's expense. "They weren't like our Negroes," the maître d' told the press in explaining why he had agreed to seat the two "African princes."

Whenever the movies *Imitation of Life* and *The Green Pastures* would be shown on TV, we watched with similar hunger—especially *Imitation of Life*. It was never on early; only the late *late* show, like the performances of Cab Calloway and Duke Ellington at the Crystal Palace. And we'd stay up. Everybody colored. The men coming home on second shift from the paper mill would stay up. Those who had to go out on the day shift and who normally would have been in bed hours earlier (because they had to be at work at 6:30) would stay up. As would we, the kids, wired for the ritual at hand. And we'd all sit in silence, fighting back the tears, watching as Delilah invents the world's greatest pancakes and a down-and-out Ned Sparks takes one taste and says, flatly, "We'll box it." Cut to a big white house, plenty of money, and Delilah saying that she doesn't want her share of the money (which should have been *all* the money); she just wants to continue to cook, clean, wash, iron, and serve her good white lady and her daughter. (Nobody in our living room was going for *that*.) And then Delilah shows up at her light-complected daughter's school one day, unexpectedly, to pick her up, and there's the daughter, Peola, ducking down behind her books, and the white teacher saying, I'm sorry, ma'am, there must be some mistake. We have no little colored children here. And then Delilah, spying her baby, says, Oh, yes you do. Peola! Peola! Come here to your mammy, honey chile. And then Peola runs out of the room, breaking her poor, sweet mother's heart. And Peola continues to break her mother's heart, by passing, leaving the race, and marrying white. Yet her mama under-stands, always understands, and, dying, makes detailed plans for her own big, beautiful funeral, complete with six white horses and a carriage and a jazz band, New Orleans style. And she dies and is about to be buried, when, out of nowhere, comes grown-up Peola, saying, "Don't die, Mama, don't die, Mama, I'm sorry, Mama, I'm sorry," and throws her light-and-bright-and-damn-near-white self onto her mama's casket. By this time, we have stopped trying to fight back the tears and are boo-hooing all over the place. Then we turn to our *own* mama and tell her how much we love her and swear that we will *never, ever* pass for white. I promise, Mama. I promise.

Peola had sold her soul to the Devil. This was the first popular Faust in the black tradition, the bargain with the Devil over the cultural soul. Talk about a cautionary tale.

The Green Pastures was an altogether more uplifting view
of things, our Afro Paradiso. Make way for the Lawd! Make
way for the Lawd! And Rex Ingram, dressed in a long black
frock coat and a long white beard, comes walking down the
Streets Paved with Gold, past the Pearly Gates, while Negroes
with the whitest wings of fluffy cotton fly around Heaven,
playing harps, singing spirituals, having fish fries, and eating
watermelon. Hard as I try, I can't stop seeing God as that
black man who played Him in *The Green Pastures* and seeing
Noah as Rochester from the Jack Benny show, trying to bargain with God to let him take along an extra keg of wine or
two.

Civil rights took us all by surprise. Every night we'd wait
until the news to see what "Dr. King and dem" were doing. It was like watching the Olympics or the World Series
when somebody colored was on. The murder of Emmett
Till was one of my first memories. He whistled at some
white girl, they said; that's all he did. He was beat so bad
they didn't even want to open the casket, but his mama made
them. She wanted the world to see what they had done to her
baby.

In 1957, when I was in second grade, black children integrated Central High School in Little Rock, Arkansas. We
watched it on TV. All of us watched it. I don't mean Mama and
Daddy and Rocky. I mean *all* the colored people in America
watched it, together, with one set of eyes. We'd watch it in
the morning, on the *Today* show on NBC, before we'd go to
school; we'd watch it in the evening, on the news, with Edward R. Murrow on CBS. We'd watch the Special Bulletins
at night, interrupting our TV shows.

The children were all well scrubbed and greased down, as
we'd say. Hair short and closely cropped, parted, and oiled
(the boys); "done" in a "permanent" and straightened, with
turned-up bangs and curls (the girls). Starched shirts, white,
and creased pants, shoes shining like a buck private's spit

shine. Those Negroes were *clean*. The fact was, those children trying to get the right to enter that school in Little Rock looked like black versions of models out of *Jack & Jill* magazine, to which my mama had subscribed for me so that I could see what children outside the Valley were up to. "They hand-picked those children," Daddy would say. "No dummies, no nappy hair, heads not too kinky, lips not too thick, no disses and no dats." At seven, I was dismayed by his cynicism. It bothered me somehow that those children would have been chosen, rather than just having shown up or volunteered or been nearby in the neighborhood.

Daddy was jaundiced about the civil rights movement, and especially about the Reverend Dr. Martin Luther King, Jr. He'd say all of his names, to drag out his scorn. By the mid-sixties, we'd argue about King from sunup to sundown. Sometimes he'd just mention King to get a rise from me, to make a sagging evening more interesting, to see if I had *learned* anything real yet, to see how long I could think up counter arguments before getting so mad that my face would turn purple. I think he just liked the color purple on my face, liked producing it there. But he was not of two minds about those children in Little Rock.

The children would get off their school bus surrounded by soldiers from the National Guard and by a field of state police. They would stop at the steps of the bus and seem to take a very deep breath. Then the phalanx would start to move slowly along this gulley of sidewalk and rednecks that connected the steps of the school bus with the white wooden double doors of the school. All kinds of crackers would be lining that gulley, separated from the phalanx of children by rows of state police, who formed a barrier arm in arm. Cheerleaders from the all-white high school that was desperately trying to stay that way were dressed in those funny little pleated skirts, with a big red C for "Central" on their chests, and they'd wave their pom-poms and start to cheer: "Two, four, six, eight—We don't want to integrate!" And all those crackers and all those rednecks would join in that chant as if their lives depended on it. Deafening, it was: even on our twelve-inch TV, a three-inch speaker buried along the back of its left side.

The TV was the ritual arena for the drama of race. In our family, it was located in the living room, where it functioned like a fireplace in the proverbial New England winter. I'd sit in the water in the galvanized tub in the middle of our kitchen, watching the TV in the next room while Mama did the laundry or some other chore as she waited for Daddy to come home from his second job. We watched people getting hosed and cracked over their heads, people being spat upon and arrested, rednecks siccing fierce dogs on women and children, our people responding by singing and marching and staying strong. Eyes on the prize. Eyes on the prize. George Wallace at the gate of the University of Alabama, blocking Autherine Lucy's way. Charlayne Hunter at the University of Georgia. President Kennedy interrupting our scheduled program with a special address, saying that James Meredith will *definitely* enter the University of Mississippi; and saying it like he believed it (unlike Ike), saying it like the big kids said "It's our turn to play" on the basketball court and walking all through us as if we weren't there.

Whatever tumult our small screen revealed, though, the dawn of the civil rights era could be no more than a spectator sport in Piedmont. It was almost like a war being fought overseas. And all things considered, white and colored Piedmont got along pretty well in those years, the fifties and early sixties. At least as long as colored people didn't try to sit down in the Cut-Rate or at the Rendezvous Bar, or eat pizza at Eddie's, or buy property, or move into the white neighborhoods, or dance with, date, or dilate upon white people. Not to mention try to get a job in the craft unions at the paper mill. Or have a drink at the white VFW, or join the white American Legion, or get loans at the bank, or just generally get out of line. Other than that, colored and white got on pretty well.

3 / Wet Dogs
& White People

You just wouldn't know it from Mama.

I remember the first time I got angry at my older daughter, Maggie. Not the angry that a parent gets when he's tired, or irritable, or stressed. But *angry*, deepdown angry, angry like: Do I know this person I've helped bring into the world and have been living with for seven or eight years? We were driving along the highway that connects Piedmont to Cumberland, and I was going on about Mama, about how she had taught me to read and write in one day in the kitchen of our second house, down Rat Tail Road. ("You want to learn how to write?" was all she had asked me. And I had said yes, so she wrote out all the letters in printing and in script, and we made them together on our red kitchen table.) And about how elegant, graceful, and beautiful she was when I was growing up.

"Too bad she was never like that when *I* knew her," Maggie called from the back seat.

It was less the words than her tone, the muted scorn with which she said she had never seen my mother as beautiful, that knocked the wind out of me. My head fell toward my chest, stopped by the top of the steering wheel. I felt my eyes blinking as I searched for breath and searched for words. I wanted to yell at her, I wanted to stop the car and shake her little shoulders and smack her little butt, I wanted to thunder at her and demand that she apologize on her dead grand-mother's grave.

Instead, tears filled my eyes as I said, "That was a terribly rude thing to say!" or some such bland parental remonstration. Then we all sat in silence as we drove on down to Cumberland, straight down Greene Street, right past the house that my great-grandparents bought in 1882, headed for the Country Club Shopping Mall by way of Hanson's drugstore, which still makes the best cherry smashes in the world. Passing the house where Daddy was raised, after his parents sold the farm at Patterson's Creek and moved the twenty or so miles into town, reminded me of Daddy's mother, Nan, or, more properly, Gertrude Helen Redman Gates. People used to talk about how beautiful she was—like a little china doll, they'd say—and she must have loved me, because she loved her seventh and youngest son, my daddy. And he worshiped her. Had I ever said anything like my Maggie just said in my car, I would have been dead, the late Skippy Gates. But I wouldn't have *said* what my daughter said, though I might have *thought* it.

And that's what I spent the time in the car on the way to get the cherry smashes thinking about. I was remembering how musty I thought Nan smelled, and how she had scraggly, yellowing gray hair, like a scarecrow with corn silk for its mane.

Then, anger melting into dizzy affection, I began to think, dotingly, about how mordant my Maggie's sense of timing had been, how deep her thoughts must be. How masterfully the blow had been delivered. How wrong I was to have been angry.

I found myself wishing, too, that Maggie could have seen

my mother when she was young and Mama and I would go to a funeral and she'd stand up to read the dead person's eulogy. She made the ignorant and ugly sound like scholars and movie stars, turned the mean and evil into saints and angels. She knew what people had meant to be in their hearts, not what the world had forced them to become. She knew the ways in which working too hard for paltry wages could turn you mean and cold, could kill that thing that had made you laugh. She remembered the way you had hoped to be, not the way you actually were. And she always got it right, even if after the funeral Daddy would wonder aloud which sonofabitch had been put in that casket instead of that simple-assed nigger So-and-so. Mama'd always laugh at that: it meant that she had been real good.

One day, Mama and I were sitting at home, like we did almost every day. She used to get *McCall's* magazine for the sewing patterns. She'd gone to seamstress school in Atlantic City, and she could sew *anything*. But *McCall's* also provided me with cutout dolls, the Betsy McCall dolls.

(I enjoyed playing with paper dolls, just as I enjoyed playing with puppets and marionettes. My all-time favorite Christmas present was a Jerry Mahoney ventriloquist dummy and a tap-dancing black minstrel known as Dancing Dan the Colored Man. I wish we had kept that thing: you sang or spoke into a microphone, and Dancing Dan's legs and feet would go this way and that, propelled by a moving platform activated by the sound of your voice.

(It never occurred to me that it was racist; I just thought it odd that he was so very dark and that his lips were so big and so red.)

Anyway, Mama and I were at home one weekday, and she was sewing on her magnificent Singer sewing machine, and Betsy and I were getting down to some serious business in the middle of our kitchen floor. The phone rang. I remember that phone because we had one just like it in every house we lived in: a solid-black kitchen wall phone, with a rotary dial that wouldn't be hurried no matter how urgently you dragged your finger.

"What?" I heard Mama gasp. "Where?"

She slammed down the phone and ran to the television in the front room. (The poetry in our lives did not extend to the naming of our rooms.) She had turned to an afternoon program called *The Big Payoff*. Just as she flipped on the show, we saw a handwritten letter being scrolled up the screen.

The letter was all about Mama!

It turns out that Mama's brother Harry had written to the producers of the show, telling them about my mother. About how she had left school at the end of junior high and gone to work to support her family—especially to put four of her brothers through college—and how she sent them money regularly, and how they would send her their dirty laundry and she would darn, wash, iron, and starch whatever appeared in those dark-brown semi-cardboard boxes that you had to tie closed with even darker-brown straps and send through the mail. And how for all these reasons, she should be selected as the winner of their write-in contest.

The phone started ringing off the hook, and all the colored people who were at home poured into Erin Street. Mama broke down and cried—and she almost never cried, not even at funerals. So I started to cry too, because I did not know what was going on. Hell, everybody else knew. "And colored too," Mr. Phil Cole, Daddy's best friend, mumbled to him later that night, after the celebrating was over and everyone else had filed out of our house. I bet they didn't know they were giving all this to a colored lady.

A week or two later, our kitchen floor was crowded with large cardboard boxes, brought by a delivery truck. I remember a gold evening dress, lots of earrings and necklaces, perfume and shoes, and a whole set of American Tourister luggage. I loved the color of that luggage, a deep luxurious tan. (The leather wore very well. I used the medium suitcase when I went off to Yale some fifteen years later.)

Mama *strutted* in those clothes. I couldn't believe that Uncle Harry had done this nice thing for Mama; he and his brothers had never done anything special for her before.

If only Maggie could have seen Mama when she'd stand up to read the minutes of the previous meeting of the PTA. Because in 1957, Mama was elected the first colored secretary of the PTA.

I used to get dressed up after dinner and walk down to the high school with Mama, over in the Orchard. I'd sit near the front so I'd get a good view, and then Betty Kimmel, the PTA president, would ask Mom to read the minutes. Mama, dressed to kill in that gold dress she'd won on *The Big Payoff*, would stand and read those minutes. It was poetry, pure poetry. She'd read each word beautifully, mellifluously, each syllable spoken roundly but without the hypercorrection of Negroes who make "again" rhyme with "rain."

Before Mama started reading the minutes, colored people never joined the PTA. But she was a leader. They still were scared, but they couldn't let Mama down. They "had to represent colored," as they'd say, and just get on with it. And so they'd dress up, too, the women, and traipse on over to the PTA, just to see Mama read her minutes, just to represent the race, just to let those white people know that we was around here too, just to be proud that one of us could do it.

No more beautiful woman existed than Mama—so it seemed to me when she read aloud her own careful script. She had shiny black sparkling eyes; a light inside would come on when she performed.

Stylish, stylish: all the men used to say that, standing on the bank corner while Mama and I walked by, heads held high, and acknowledging the riffraff without being too interested or too rude about it. My mama *knew* she looked good.

As a child, I was secure in her knowledge of things, of how to *do* things and function in the world, of how to *be* in the world and command respect. In her courage I was safe. She was not afraid of dogs, like I was, not even Brownie, the Drains' spaniel, or Spotty, the Wilsons' crazy barker, or even Mugsy, the brindle who, standing on his two hind legs, had ripped open the shoulder of my flight jacket when I was eight.

But most important of all, for Piedmont and for me, she did not seem to fear white people.

She simply hated them, hated them with a passion she seldom disclosed.

There were rare occasions when I would look into her face and see a stranger. In 1959, when I was nine, Mike Wallace and CBS aired a documentary about Black Muslims. It was called "The Hate That Hate Produced," and these were just about the scariest black people I'd ever seen. Black people who talked right into the faces of white people, telling them off without even blinking. While I sat cowering in our living room, I happened to glance over at my mother. A certain radiance was slowly transforming her soft brown face, as she listened to Malcolm X naming the white man the Devil. "Amen," she said, quietly at first. "All right now," she continued, much more heatedly. All this time, and I hadn't known just how deeply my mother despised white people. It was like watching the Wicked Witch of the West emerge out of the transforming features of Dorothy. The revelation was both terrifying and thrilling.

The same thing would happen several years later when the Martin Luther King riots were shown on television. The first colored secretary of the Piedmont PTA watched the flames with dancing eyes.

But Mama was practical as well as proud. Her attitude was that she and Daddy would provide the best for us, so that no white person could put us down or keep us out for reasons of appearance, color aside. The rest was up to us, once we got in those white places. Like school, which desegregated without a peep in 1955, the year before I started first grade. Otherwise she didn't care to live in white neighborhoods or be around white people.

White people, she said, were *dirty*: They tasted right out of pots on the stove. Only some kind of animal, or the lowest order of trash, would ever taste out of a pot on the stove. Anybody with manners knew that; even colored people without manners knew that. It was *white* people who didn't know that. If you are cooking, Mama would say, and want to check your seasoning, take the big wooden spoon you use for stirring, place some stew or whatever it is in a cup or small bowl, and then, with a separate spoon or fork, have a taste. Tasting right out of a pot was almost as bad as drinking after somebody, on the same side of the cup or glass, or right after them on a Coca-Cola bottle without wiping their lips off real good. "I'd rather go *thirsty* myself," Uncle Raymond would say. By the mid-sixties, he was also given to pronouncing: "I'd rather white people call me a *nigger* than call me black." If he'd had to choose between being called black and drinking out of the same bottle after another human being, I'm not sure what Uncle Raymond would have done.

One thing we always did was smell good, partly because we liked scents, but partly because white people said we smelled bad *naturally*, like we had some sort of odor gene. "Here come you niggers, funking up the place"—even we'd crack that kind of joke a lot. So one thing colored people *had* to do around white people was smell good. And not have ash on our elbows or knees. Crust, we called it. Moisturizing cream was "crust eradicator," and Mama made sure we always brought some when we went over to the swimming pool, so as not to Embarrass the Race.

But it was white people who smelled bad, Mama always said. When they got wet. When they get wet, she said, they smell like dogs.

I do hate the smell of a wet dog, I have to confirm. But I don't think white people smell like that when their hair is wet, and I have done a lot of sniffing of wet-headed white people in my time. At first, as a child, I had a mission to test my mama's hypothesis:

"Hello, my name is Skipper. I'm taking a survey. . . . Could I smell your wet hair?"

Actually, my technique was subtler, though only slightly.

I remember sidling up to my favorite classmate, Linda Hoffman, one day at the swimming pool—which had integrated in that same year, 1956—nostrils flared, trying to breathe in as deeply as I could, prepared for the worst. "What's wrong with you?" she asked, suspiciously. "Uh, rose fever," I said.

She didn't believe me.

And my mother would not have believed the result of my researches, even had I shared them with her. That these doggy-smelling white people should cast olfactory aspersions upon *us* was bitter gall for her.

Yet if the anxiety about stereotype made colored Piedmont a generally sweet-smelling lot, there was a very significant exception, one that pertains to the mystery surrounding one of Piedmont's singular attractions—Dent Davis's aforementioned Famous Homemade Ring Bologna.

Davis's delectable bologna was dark red, with a tight, crimson, translucent skin, and was sold in rings at Davis's Bakery, downtown on Ashfield Street. Dent was German, or so we believed, and he ran the shop with his two middle-aged daughters. Each had her dark hair in a bun, always "done"—as women, for some reason, still say—and one of them, Matilda, always wore luscious red lipstick. She was not a pretty woman, perhaps, but with her light-beige powdered cheeks, her dark-brown, almost black hair and dark-brown eyes, and that red lipstick, when she stood before the golden and dark-brown breads, cookies, and pastries, or wrapped the blood-red links of her daddy's bologna in white waxed butcher's paper with that deliberate way she had, she was, I was convinced, one of the loveliest creatures on God's green earth.

However delicious our tap water, however delicious our local brand of syrup, none of these delicacies of the Potomac Valley tasted better than fried pieces of Dent's bologna. For Dent Davis had a secret ingredient, whose nature nobody has ever ascertained. And I mean nobody.

Nobody white, that is.

Because all the colored people in Piedmont attributed the special taste and texture to Mr. Boxie, Dent Davis's faithful colored handyman, who had Dent's trust and faith, possessed the keys to his shop and house, and was always on hand, even when Davis locked everyone else out so he could make up a batch of that secret bologna.

What's in that bologna? the colored men would ask Mr. Boxie.

Can't say, he'd reply, with a wry twist of his lips. Can't say.

That nigger knows what's in that bologna, the town—*our* town—would whisper. Wonder if Dent lets him help make it?

The town's concern with Dent's liberality in relation to Mr. Boxie had nothing to do with the fact that Dent Davis was German and Mr. Boxie was colored, and the year was 1955 or so, when the words "civil rights" were about to become current. Boxie was Dent's *man*, so all of that was by-the-by. The town's concern was that Mr. Boxie was the dirtiest, smelliest, sloppiest, most disheveled colored man in all of Piedmont, and maybe the world. Mr. Boxie put the *un* in unkempt. The town said Mr. Boxie was *funky*, long before Motown or James Brown thought of making "funky" mean cool, hip, or "down." No, Mr. Boxie was funky because he smelled bad.

"A whiff of Boxcars," Big Mom, Mama's mama, would say, "would knock even a grown man out." And to think that Mr. Boxie was the chief chef in the making of Piedmont's sole contribution to the world's culinary chef d'oeuvre was more than I—once I had confirmed the rumor's truth beyond the wrought-iron railings of the elementary-school courtyard—could bear.

Tell me it ain't so, Pop, I said to my father. It's so, boy. It was true, then: the funk was what did it. It was a long time before I'd try Dent Davis's bologna again, enriched as I now knew it to be by Mr. Boxie's stench. And I *never* again tried it raw. Fried, however, was another matter. Gas will kill *anything*, Aunt Marguerite said to me one day as I eyed my dinner plate balefully, wanting so much to be able to forget the loathsome origins of this delicacy that she had placed before me. Anything, she insisted. I managed to smile at her between mouthfuls, after the first full swallow stayed down.

White people couldn't cook; everybody knew that. Which made it a puzzle why such an important part of the civil rights movement had to do with integrating restaurants and lunch counters. The food wasn't any good anyway. Principle of the thing, Daddy's buddy Mr. Ozzie Washington would assert. They don't know nothin' about seasoning, my aunt Marguerite would say. I like my food seasoned, she'd add.

If there is a key to unlocking the culinary secrets of the

Coleman family, it is that a slab of fatback or a cupful of bacon drippings or a couple of ham hocks and a long simmering time are absolutely essential to a well-cooked vegetable. Cook it till it's *done,* Mama would say. Cook it till it's dead, we'd learn to say much later. When I first tasted a steamed vegetable, I thought it was raw. The Colemans were *serious* about their cooking and their eating. There was none of this eating on the run; meals lasted for hours, with lots of good conversation thrown in. The happiest I ever saw my aunts and uncles in the Coleman family was when they'd slowly eat their savory meals, washing everything down with several glasses of iced tea. Especially at the Family Reunion, or on Christmas Day up at Big Mom's house. "Eating good"—with plenty of fat and cholesterol—was held to be essential to proper health and peace of mind.

There were plenty of Colemans: nine brothers—known as "the boys"—and four sisters, the youngest of whom had died when she was a day or two old. (There's enough niggers in your mother's family, Daddy would remark, to cast a Tarzan movie.)

Sunday in Piedmont was everybody's favorite day, because you could eat yourself silly, starting just after church. Mama didn't go to church on Sundays, except to read out her obituaries. She'd cook while we were at Sunday school. Rarely did the menu vary: fried chicken, mashed potatoes, baked corn (corn pudding), green beans and potatoes (with lots of onions and bacon drippings and a hunk of ham), gravy, rolls, and a salad of iceberg lettuce, fresh tomatoes (grown in Uncle Jim's garden), a sliced boiled egg, scallions, and Wishbone's Italian dressing. We'd eat Mama's Sunday dinners in the middle of the day and keep nibbling for the rest of the afternoon and evening. White people just can't cook good, Aunt Marguerite used to say; that's why they need to hire us.

4 / In the Kitchen

We always had a gas stove in the kitchen, though
electric cooking became fashionable in Piedmont,
like using Crest toothpaste rather than Colgate, or
watching Huntley and Brinkley rather than Walter Cronkite.
But for us it was gas, Colgate, and good ole Walter Cronkite,
come what may. We used gas partly out of loyalty to Big Mom,
Mama's mama, because she was mostly blind and still loved
to cook, and she could feel her way better with gas than with
electric.

But the most important thing about our gas-equipped
kitchen was that Mama used to do hair there. She had a "hot
comb"—a fine-toothed iron instrument with a long wooden
handle—and a pair of iron curlers that opened and closed like
scissors: Mama would put them into the gas fire until they
glowed. You could smell those prongs heating up.

I liked what that smell meant for the shape of my day. There
was an intimate warmth in the women's tones as they talked
with my mama while she did their hair. I knew what the
women had been through to get their hair ready to be "done,"
because I would watch Mama do it to herself. How that

scorched kink could be transformed through grease and fire into a magnificent head of wavy hair was a miracle to me. Still is.

Mama would wash her hair over the sink, a towel wrapped round her shoulders, wearing just her half-slip and her white bra. (We had no shower until we moved down Rat Tail Road into Doc Wolverton's house, in 1954.) After she had dried it, she would grease her scalp thoroughly with blue Bergamot hair grease, which came in a short, fat jar with a picture of a beautiful colored lady on it. It's important to grease your scalp real good, my mama would explain, to keep from burning yourself.

Of course, her hair would return to its natural kink almost as soon as the hot water and shampoo hit it. To me, it was another miracle how hair so "straight" would so quickly become kinky again once it even approached some water.

My mama had only a few "clients" whose heads she "did"— and did, I think, because she enjoyed it, rather than for the few dollars it brought in. They would sit on one of our red plastic kitchen chairs, the kind with the shiny metal legs, and brace themselves for the process. Mama would stroke that red-hot iron, which by this time had been in the gas fire for half an hour or more, slowly but firmly through their hair, from scalp to strand's end. It made a scorching, crinkly sound, the hot iron did, as it burned its way through damp kink, leaving in its wake the straightest of hair strands, each of them standing up long and tall but drooping at the end, like the top of a heavy willow tree. Slowly, steadily, with deftness and grace, Mama's hands would transform a round mound of Odetta kink into a darkened swamp of everglades. The Bergamot made the hair shiny; the heat of the hot iron gave it a brownish-red cast. Once all the hair was as straight as God allows kink to get, Mama would take the well-heated curling iron and twirl the straightened strands into more or less loosely wrapped curls. She claimed that she owed her strength and skill as a hairdresser to her wrists, and her little finger would poke out the way it did when she sipped tea. Mama was a southpaw, who wrote upside down and backwards to produce the cleanest, roundest letters you've ever seen.

The "kitchen" she would all but remove from sight with a pair of shears bought for this purpose. Now, the *kitchen* was the room in which we were sitting, the room where Mama did hair and washed clothes, and where each of us bathed in a galvanized tub. But the word has another meaning, and the "kitchen" I'm speaking of now is the very kinky bit of hair at the back of the head, where the neck meets the shirt collar. If there ever was one part of our African past that resisted assimilation, it was the kitchen. No matter how hot the iron, no matter how powerful the chemical, no matter how stringent the mashed-potatoes-and-lye formula of a man's "process," neither God nor woman nor Sammy Davis, Jr., could straighten the kitchen. The kitchen was permanent, irredeemable, invincible kink. Unassimilably African. No matter what you did, no matter how hard you tried, nothing could dekink a person's kitchen. So you trimmed it off as best you could.

When hair had begun to "turn," as they'd say, or return to its natural kinky glory, it was the kitchen that turned first. When the kitchen started creeping up the back of the neck, it was time to get your hair done again. The kitchen around the back, and nappy edges at the temples.

Sometimes, after dark, Mr. Charlie Carroll would come to have his hair done. Mr. Charlie Carroll was very light-complected and had a ruddy nose, the kind of nose that made me think of Edmund Gwenn playing Kris Kringle in *Miracle on 34th Street*. At the beginning, they did it after Rocky and I had gone to sleep. It was only later that we found out he had come to our house so Mama could iron his hair—not with a hot comb and curling iron but with our very own Proctor-Silex steam iron. For some reason, Mr. Charlie would conceal his Frederick Douglass mane under a big white Stetson hat, which I never saw him take off. Except when he came to our house, late at night, to have his hair pressed.

(Later, Daddy would tell us about Mr. Charlie's most prized piece of knowledge, which the man would confide only after his hair had been pressed, as a token of intimacy. "Not many people know this," he'd say in a tone of circumspection, "but George Washington was Abraham Lincoln's daddy." Nodding solemnly, he'd add the clincher: "A white man told me." Though he was in dead earnest, this became a humorous refrain around the house—"a white man told me"—used to punctuate especially preposterous assertions.)

My mother furtively examined my daughters' kitchens whenever we went home for a visit in the early eighties. It became a game between us. I had told her not to do it, because I didn't like the politics it suggested of "good" and "bad" hair. "Good" hair was straight. "Bad" hair was kinky. Even in the late sixties, at the height of Black Power, most people could not bring themselves to say "bad" for "good" and "good" for "bad." They still said that hair like white hair was "good," even if they encapsulated it in a disclaimer like "what we used to call 'good.'"

Maggie would be seated in her high chair, throwing food this way and that, and Mama would be cooing about how cute it all was, remembering how I used to do the same thing, and wondering whether Maggie's flinging her food with her left hand meant that she was going to be a southpaw too. When my daughter was just about covered with Franco-American SpaghettiOs, Mama would seize the opportunity and wipe her clean, dipping her head, tilted to one side, down under the back of Maggie's neck. Sometimes, if she could get away with it, she'd even rub a curl between her fingers, just to make sure that her bifocals had not deceived her. Then she'd sigh with satisfaction and relief, thankful that her prayers had been answered. No kink . . . yet. "Mama!" I'd shout, pretending to be angry. (Every once in a while, if no one was looking, I'd peek too.)

I say "yet" because most black babies are born with soft, silken hair. Then, sooner or later, it begins to "turn," as inevitably as do the seasons or the leaves on a tree. And if it's meant to turn, it *turns*, no matter how hard you try to stop it. People once thought baby oil would stop it. They were wrong.

Everybody I knew as a child wanted to have good hair. You could be as ugly as homemade sin dipped in misery and still be thought attractive if you had good hair. Jesus Moss was what the girls at Camp Lee, Virginia, had called Daddy's hair during World War II. I know he played that thick head of hair for all it was worth, too. Still would, if he could.

My own hair was "not a bad grade," as barbers would tell me when they cut my head for the first time. It's like a doctor reporting the overall results of the first full physical that he has given you. "You're in good shape" or "Blood pressure's kind of high; better cut down on salt."

I spent much of my childhood and adolescence messing with my hair. I definitely wanted straight hair. Like Pop's.

When I was about three, I tried to stick a wad of Bazooka bubble gum to that straight hair of his. I suppose what fixed that memory for me is the spanking I got for doing so: he turned me upside down, holding me by my feet, the better to paddle my behind. Little *nigger*, he shouted, walloping away. I started to laugh about it two days later, when my behind stopped hurting.

When black people say "straight," of course, they don't usually mean "straight" literally, like, say, the hair of Peggy Lipton (the white girl on *The Mod Squad*) or Mary of Peter,

Paul and Mary fame; black people call that "stringy" hair. No, "straight" just means not kinky, no matter what contours the curl might take. Because Daddy had straight hair, I would have done *anything* to have straight hair—and I used to try everything to make it straight, short of getting a process, which only riffraff were dumb enough to do.

Of the wide variety of techniques and methods I came to master in the great and challenging follicle prestidigitation, almost all had two things in common: a heavy, oil-based grease and evenly applied pressure. It's no accident that many of the biggest black companies in the fifties and sixties made hair products. Indeed, we do have a vast array of hair grease. And I have tried it all, in search of that certain silky touch, one that leaves neither the hand nor the pillow sullied by grease.

I always wondered what Frederick Douglass put on *his* hair, or Phillis Wheatley. Or why Wheatley has that rag on her head in the little engraving in the frontispiece of her book. One thing is for sure: you can bet that when Wheatley went to England to see the Countess of Huntington, she did not stop by the Queen's Coiffeur on the way. So many black people still get their hair straightened that it's a wonder we don't have a national holiday for Madame C. J. Walker, who invented the process for straightening kinky hair, rather than for Dr. King. Jheri-curled or "relaxed"—it's still fried hair.

I used all the greases, from sea-blue Bergamot, to creamy vanilla Duke (in its orange-and-white jar), to the godfather of grease, the formidable Murray's. Now, Murray's was some *serious* grease. Whereas Bergamot was like oily Jell-O and Duke was viscous and sickly sweet, Murray's was light brown and *hard*. Hard as lard and twice as greasy, Daddy used to say whenever the subject of Murray's came up. Murray's came in an orange can with a screw-on top. It was so hard that some people would put a match to the can, just to soften it and make it more manageable. In the late sixties, when Afros came into style, I'd use Afro-Sheen. From Murray's to Duke to Afro-Sheen: that was my progression in black consciousness.

We started putting hot towels or washrags over our greased-down Murray's-coated heads, in order to melt the wax into the scalp and follicles. Unfortunately, the wax had a curious habit of running down your neck, ears, and forehead. Not to mention your pillowcase.

Another problem was that if you put two palmfuls of Murray's on your head, your hair turned white. Duke did the same thing. It was a challenge: if you got rid of the white stuff, you had a magnificent head of wavy hair. Murray's turned kink into waves. Lots of waves. Frozen waves. A hurricane couldn't have blown those waves around.

That was the beauty of it. Murray's was so hard that it froze your hair into the wavy style you brushed it into. It looked really good if you wore a part. A lot of guys had parts *cut* into their hair by a barber, with clippers or a straight-edge razor. Especially if you had kinky hair—in which case you'd generally wear a short razor cut, or what we called a Quo Vadis.

Being obsessed with our hair, we tried to be as innovative as possible. Everyone knew about using a stocking cap, because your father or your uncle or the older guys wore them whenever something really big was about to happen, secular or sacred, a funeral or a dance, a wedding or a trip in which you confronted official white people, or when you were trying to look really sharp. When it was time to be clean, you wore a stocking cap. If the event was really a big one, you made a new cap for the occasion.

A stocking cap was made by asking your mother for one of her hose, and cutting it with a pair of scissors about six inches or so from the open end, where the elastic goes up to the top of the thigh. Then you'd knot the cut end, and behold—a conical-shaped hat or cap, with an elastic band that you pulled down low on your forehead and down around your neck in the back. A good stocking cap, to work well, had to fit tight and snug, like a press. And it had to fit that tightly because it *was* a press: it pressed your hair with the force of the hose's elastic. If you greased your hair down real good and left the stocking cap on long enough—*voilà*: you got a head of pressed-against-the-scalp waves. If you used Murray's, and if you wore a stocking cap to sleep, you got a *whole lot* of waves. (You also got a ring around your forehead when you woke up, but eventually that disappeared.)

And then you could enjoy your concrete 'do. Swore we were bad, too, with all that grease and those flat heads. My brother and I would brush it out a bit in the morning, so it would look—ahem—"natural."

Grown men still wear stocking caps, especially older men, who generally keep their caps in their top drawer, along with their cuff links and their see-through silk socks, their Maverick tie, their silk handkerchief, and whatever else they prize most.

A Murrayed-down stocking cap was the respectable version of the process, which, by contrast, was most definitely not a cool thing to have, at least if you weren't an entertainer by trade.

Zeke and Keith and Poochie and a few other stars of the basketball team all used to get a process once or twice a year. It was expensive, and to get one you had to go to Pittsburgh or D.C. or Uniontown, someplace where there were enough colored people to support a business. They'd disappear, then reappear a day or two later, strutting like peacocks, their hair burned slightly red from the chemical lye base. They'd also wear "rags" or cloths or handkerchiefs around it when they slept or played basketball. Do-rags, they were called. But the result was *straight* hair, with a hint of wave. No curl. Do-it-yourselfers took their chances at home with a concoction of mashed potatoes and lye.

The most famous process, outside of what Malcolm X describes in his *Autobiography* and maybe that of Sammy Davis, Jr., was Nat King Cole's. Nat King Cole had patent-leather hair.

"That man's got the finest process money can buy." That's what Daddy said the night Cole's TV show aired on NBC, November 5, 1956. I remember the date because everyone came to our house to watch it and to celebrate one of Daddy's buddies' birthdays. Yeah, Uncle Joe chimed in, they can do shit to his hair that the average Negro can't even *think* about— secret shit.

Nat King Cole was *clean*. I've had an ongoing argument with a Nigerian friend about Nat King Cole for twenty years now. Not whether or not he could sing; any fool knows that he could sing. But whether or not he was a handkerchief-head for wearing that patent-leather process.

Sammy Davis's process I detested. It didn't look good on him. Worse still, he liked to have a fried strand dangling down the middle of his forehead, shaking it out from the crown when he sang. But Nat King Cole's hair was a thing unto itself, a beautifully sculpted work of art that he and he alone should have had the right to wear.

The only difference between a process and a stocking cap, really, was taste; yet Nat King Cole—unlike, say, Michael Jackson—looked *good* in his process. His head looked like Rudolph Valentino's in the twenties, and some say it was Valentino that the process imitated. But Nat King Cole wore a process because it suited his face, his demeanor, his name, his style. He was as clean as he wanted to be.

I had forgotten all about Nat King Cole and that patent-leather look until the day in 1971 when I was sitting in an Arab restaurant on the island of Zanzibar, surrounded by men in fezzes and white caftans, trying to learn how to eat curried goat and rice with the fingers of my right hand, feeling two million miles from home, when all of a sudden the old transistor radio sitting on top of a china cupboard stopped blaring out its Swahili music to play "Fly Me to the Moon" by Nat King Cole. The restaurant's din was not affected at all, not even by half a decibel. But in my mind's eye, I saw it: the King's sleek black magnificent tiara. I managed, barely, to blink back the tears.

II / Family Pictures

5 / Up the Hill

When we were growing up, being a Coleman was a very big deal in Piedmont. My uncles and aunts were very well thought of; most went as far at the paper mill as a colored man could go, in their respective trades, once the mill decided to allow blacks out of the loaders. The Colemans were the first colored to own guns and hunt on white land, the first to become Eagle Scouts, the first to go to college, the first to own property.

And at the head of the Coleman clan, when I was young, was Big Mom, my mother's mother, also known as Biggie. She was a figure of reverence and fascination, but most of all, whenever any of her children did not want you to do something, she was a figurative agent of social control.

Big Mom was astoundingly religious. I mean, if there is a Heaven, then Big Mom has *got* to be in it: you can have no doubt about that. Big Mom went to church *every* Sunday. She prayed a lot, and she never went anywhere, at least in my lifetime, except to the doctor and to church. She had started to lose her sight by the time I was a boy, though she could see you close up. Big Mom was always in the kitchen or in the dining room, perched in front of the big picture window that her youngest son, Earkie, had installed when eventually he was allowed to buy Big Mom's house from the Fredlocks, the white people who owned the funeral home over in the Orchard. She called me "Skippy Boy" or "Skipper Ripper Dipper," and spoke with me, rather than merely silently acknowledging another of her nameless, countless grandchildren. And she seemed genuinely to like me, which is the only reason I would have taken all those breathless steps to climb "Up the Hill" to Big Mom's house.

My cousins, my uncountable cousins, all venerated Big Mom, but like "a Virgin Mary image in a church," as Zora Neale Hurston put it. I liked her partly because I could make her laugh. I enjoyed teasing her about running around with Mr. Toots, or dancing with Mr. Lynn or Mr. Russell down at the colored Legion on Saturday night. She'd laugh real hard at that last one, her bright-pink toothless gums revealed by the pulled-back lips of her laughter. She didn't wear her teeth around the house, saved them for church or the doctor's. I'd push up against the limits, the boundaries of the allowable things for a devilish grandson to whisper in his pious grandmother's ear. And somehow I only rarely made her mad, almost never crossed that invisible line. She knew I respected her. I liked her too, when her all-too-reverent sons were not around to cramp my style and turn her into one of those brightly painted plaster statues over at the Catholic church in Westernport.

I liked her even more when I found out why she was so holy, why she prayed so much, why she was forever asking God to forgive her her terrible sins, and why she always felt impure. There are things I've done, she'd say to my daddy, her voice trailing off. He'd say Miss Maggie, you *know* you're a good person.

It turns out that Big Mom had two lovers in her long ago

youth. One was Daddy Paul, and one was ole Griff Bruce.
Now, the rest of what I'm about to tell you was the darkest,
deepest family secret in the history of the Coleman family—
and we had some good secrets! Strange children showed up
at Big Mom's once or twice, with well-dressed colored ladies
holding their hands, trying to introduce them to their "grand-
mother," while my mother was busy trying to call a taxi—
"Just as soon as you can possibly get up here . . . Yes, that's
right . . . Coleman . . . *Coleman* . . . The green house at the
top of the hill. Right away!"—all the while using her body
and free arm to obstruct from Biggie's line of sight this finely
dressed woman with her hair all nicely greased and done, and
this little light-brown child, his hair greased down lightly and
the part cut properly in an exact straight line on the right side
of a not-too-nappy head, dressed in beige shorts, yellow shirt,
bow tie, and a jacket to match the shorts, shoes shined, dark
brown, with mulatto shoelaces, all of it bought for this monu-
mental encounter. "Lady, I'm sorry," Mama would say, "but
you got to *go*," ushering her gently, politely, but firmly out
the door and down all those wooden steps that connected Big
Mom's swinged porch to the concrete pavement in front of
her tenants, the Walkers, below.

Who was that, Mama? I'd ask in feigned innocence, wide-
eyed at how much that kid had reminded me of one of Mama's
brothers. She had the wrong house, baby, was all that Mama
would say. Then I heard Mama call one of her brothers on the
telephone after she'd shooed me into the kitchen with Big
Mom.

As luck would have it, Big Mom herself had picked as the
father of her child a man who turned out not to be the father of
her child. It was between Daddy Paul and ole Griff Bruce.
Fifty-fifty ain't good odds. Now, according to legend—and this
of course I can't verify, since the source was not a Coleman but
Daddy's oldest brother, Uncle Lawrence, and how *he* knew

I'll never know—Big Mom went to Griff Bruce and said that she was going to have a baby and that she'd take him if he got rid of his hunting dogs. Griff was a legendary hunter up Williamsport, and if Piedmont was a village, I don't know what Williamsport could have been, since Piedmont was New York City next to the dusty crossroads with a railroad-track sign that indicated that the municipality of Williamsport existed. (I never saw more than one house in Williamsport, and that was Granny's house, the house where Big Mom was born.)

Well, faced with a choice between those hunting dogs and Big Mom (not to mention Uncle Jim, in the hopper), Griff settled for what he knew and wished Big Mom well in her new life. So she married Daddy Paul. Daddy Paul was dark, with short kinky hair and a straight nose, a certain sense of bearing and of presence. His firstborn child was short, stocky, ruddy in complexion, like the Howards and the Bruces. (Big Mom was a Howard and a Clifford, families who had intermarried with white people and a few genuine Indians for a long time up in those hollows that constitute Williamsport, as well as with each other. If strange things happen at watering holes, as Aristotle said, then things just as strange happen in hollows.) The child had a natural-born capacity to love and hunt and be part of the woods. He also had an uncanny affinity for and knowledge of hunting dogs. And if all that was not enough, he looked like Griff Bruce's clone. Like Griff had spat him out, Uncle Lawrence said.

There Griff was, staring at me in Uncle Jim's face all those years, Daddy said, and I didn't even see it. But once his brother Lawrence told him, it was clear. No denying him.

That was the thing about overhearing genealogical conversations in the colored VFW. Once Pop or Mr. Roebuck Johnson made a pronouncement, the evidence was generally as plain as the nose on your face—or some kid's whose daddy wasn't his daddy and the whole town knew. To tell the truth, the colored people in Piedmont—men and women, young and old—spent a lot of time talking about sex in general and a fair amount of time detailing the exploits of the midnight warriors who were "sneakin' and creepin'," as we'd say.

It was an epidemic when I was a kid in the fifties—the talk, anyway, including talk about sex with white people, the holiest taboo. How white people couldn't know, I'll never be able to figure out, because everybody colored talked about it all day long. I guess the thing about living in a village at the foot of a mountain is that the world for you becomes, without thinking about it, self-contained. People are of two kinds, really: from the Valley, and from Elsewhere. And there is not a whole lot to keep you occupied. You could play baseball in the summer and basketball year round. You could hunt in the winter, fish in the summer. You could go to the colored Legion, to colored holiday dances. . . . And you could do the nacky-nacky. For a town with two thousand people, it seemed, there was a whole lot of nacky-nacky, colored and white.

Uncle Joe once told Daddy that he never had *seen* a place where people slept around so much or so openly as they did in Piedmont. *Goddamn*, Daddy would repeat, his voice rising squeakily and irritably high to mimic Uncle Joe's when he is drunk. Goddamn.

As I said, there's just not a lot to do in a small town. And most people there never did mind too much about fornication as a sin, or getting pregnant out of wedlock. Which is not to say that everyone had a healthy, or satisfying, sex life. It is only to say that just about everyone seemed to be sleeping with somebody, or at least that just about everyone spent lots and lots of time talking about sleeping with somebody.

I never saw nothin' at all like Piedmont, Uncle Joe would repeat, shaking his head. They just sleep together all out in the open.

Seeing the twelve Coleman children sitting together (as

they did at Christmas dinner Up the Hill at Big Mom's or at the annual Family Reunion in late July) confirmed why Africans in the New World soon came to be called colored people. Their colors ran the full spectrum of brown, like the whole race in miniature, from the richest dark chocolate to the creamiest café au lait.

The Colemans were colored people. In chronological order, as in Leviticus, Uncle Jim, or Nemo, was slightly reddish, with a big round head, a heavy build, a short, wide nose, and thin lips. Like all his brothers and sisters, he inherited Big Mom's tiny moles, which develop with age into blotchy skin.

Ed was lighter than Jim, still reddish, though, with a squarer face, high cheekbones, large squinty eyes, closely set. He had a long, straight nose, thin lips, and an even complexion. He was the tallest of the brothers, the wealthiest, and the first to own his own home.

Howard was sleepy-eyed, with a placid face, a long, straight nose, a square jaw, a high forehead, and large eyes. Charles had dark skin, a perfectly round head, wide nose, high cheekbones, lips thicker than the rest of his brothers.

Raymond was a saturated reddish-brown color, and he had a round face with evenly spaced features, his nose short and straight, his eyes smallish. He had the kinkiest hair and was the darkest, which was a source of pain for him for much of my life at least. And the Black Is Beautiful movement didn't seem to help him all that much. To his chagrin, his baby brother, David, had the lightest skin of all and the longest face. David—known as Earkie—was a handsome man, with his aquiline nose and smooth tan skin, his perpetually knitted brows over sad eyes, and his square chin.

Aunt Marguerite and Aunt Loretta had intense eyes with dark circles around them. Aunt Marguerite's eyes were open, bearing a smart expression. Ham was a caffè latté color, almost orange, and Alvin, the college professor, was a luxurious mahogany. Harry, the "legitimate" preacher (both Nemo and Earkie would get the "call" from God, near retirement time), was a cherrywood brown.

Of all my mama's nine brothers, it was Uncle Earkie with whom I had the most difficult relationship. Not only was he good-looking; he was a sharp dresser and always had a nice new car. A Riviera, say, or an Impala. Not a Pontiac or a Chevy or an Oldsmobile, like everybody else. Earkie had style.

He also had a chip on his shoulder, for reasons that I never really understood . . . until Mama said one day that her father, Daddy Paul, used to beat him, his twelfth child, unmercifully all the time when he was little and accuse him of being someone else's child.

It made me hate my father, Mama would sometimes say. He was a mean man, I guess. Not mean to Mama. But mean to Earkie. And to Uncle Ed too, his first legitimate child. We called him Peck because his initials were P. E. C., for Paul Edwin Coleman. She would tell me about a particular beating that Daddy Paul inflicted upon Uncle Peck, about how horrible it was. Once or twice she'd even cry about it. Years later, when my mother died, we found a diary she had kept in the thirties. On November 28, 1934, when she was eighteen, she had written:

This occurred on the eve of Thanksgiving, November 1934: my father must be the meanest man in this town. After whipping my brother to the skin for stealing coal, until he couldn't beat him any longer, he comes downstairs and slaps my mother in the face as hard as he can because she says to my brother "Don't let him beat you in the face." He doesn't know how to whip a child: He knocks them like dogs. God help him. Then he tells us that we can all go to hell for all he cares. . . . He says if

any of us ever turns on him, he will knock us for a row
of Sundays. Some day, we are going to do just that.

Earkie still talks about Daddy Paul like he was Solomon,
Moses, and the Good Lord Jesus, all rolled into one, just as
all his children do except Uncle Harry. I never knew Daddy
Paul, since he died at the end of the war, five years before I
was born. I only know him through Mama's stories about
Earkie. And through that diary entry.

Daddy Paul had standing in the community. "He was a
good man," people would say of him, including white people.
But his vocation was no more exalted than others'. He worked
as a janitor and handyman at the Devon Club, the mill's dry
goods store, and raising twelve children on a handyman's
salary was a stretch. Never having quite enough—whether
food or anything else—was the condition of their childhood,
and it marked them all, in different ways.

But Earkie, born almost twenty years after his eldest
brother, was marked in yet another way, as he took the beating
for an event over which he had no control. Those beatings
didn't stop him from becoming a lover, though.

Most people in Piedmont kept their dogs chained to dog-
houses in their backyards. In the middle of the night, you
could hear them barking, as somebody sneakin' and creepin'
would steal his way through the darkness into somebody else's
bedroom. The chief cause of all that nighttime barking, at
least when I was young, was my uncle Earkie, so people said.

Miss Lizzy Johnson's dogs especially would go crazy every
night when one of my uncles, baby-sitting at Big Mom's house,
would creep down the back stairs and try to sneak past those
sleeping dogs to his girlfriend's house. If my uncle had been
Jim, with Griff's hunting genes, the boy *might* have made it.
But dogs, after all, have keen ears.

Years later, my friends and I nicknamed him the Sneakin'

Deacon. He had joined Uncle Jim's Homemade Baptist Church, declared himself to be both "saved" and a deacon, and kept right on waking Miss Lizzy's hunting dogs every night on his way to visit his friend and keep her company, holding hands and quite possibly talking about the Lord, before he finally got married.

When I was nine or ten, the Coleman Family Reunion was the social event of the season. The only problem was that you had to be a Coleman to be on the list—or else be specially invited. And being invited was one big deal. Even if you were an in-law, you still weren't a Coleman. The Hills, the Stewarts, not to mention the Gateses—these weren't Colemans, at least not according to "the boys," the nine male descendants of Paul Coleman, almost all of whom named one son Paul. (My brother's name is Paul, cousin Greg's middle name is Paul, Uncle Alvin's son is named Paul, even Uncle Jim's younger son is named Paul. I could go on.) That man had power; he perpetuates himself from the grave.

As years went by, I grew more critical, deciding that I was more like the Gateses than the Colemans—a world of difference. Accordingly, I decided that Mama must have been a Howard or a Clifford, because she was totally unlike her sisters and brothers.

The Colemans weren't good storytellers, like my daddy was. They didn't drink, they didn't smoke, and if they weren't especially religious, they were especially self-righteous.

And they had ideas about a woman's place that I knew, even as a child, just were not going to play. One wanted his woman to be home all day long, waiting for him, baking bread and stuff, "so that I smell it when my foot hits the door." We used to wonder if he should try to clone Barbara Eden in *I Dream of Jeannie*, because that's about what he'd need.

They didn't exactly practice sexual equality in that family. Up at Big Mom's, on Christmas, the men would be seated

first, at the formal dining table with the extra leaves, while
the women served them. They even served the *boys* first,
before they returned to the kitchen to eat their own supper,
with Big Mom. Then they'd clear the tables and wash up. The
men retired to the living room, to watch football and chew on
the facts of life, sipping iced tea diluted with fast-melting but
regularly replenished cubes of ice, a wedge of lemon hooked
on the glass's side.

Nobody thought anything about this arrangement until I
brought my wife, Sharon, to dinner up there in 1973. When
she sat down at the table with the men, you could have heard
a pin drop. But the women served her, too, while the Coleman
boys bumbled around, trying to figure out what to say, "skin-
ning 'em back," as Pop says when black people Tom up to
white people, saying hee-hee-hee a lot.

That was our last Christmas dinner Up the Hill at Big
Mom's.

Colemans didn't hang out with other colored people very
much. Classed off, as the tradition says. You'd never find a
Coleman at the colored VFW. Come to that, I never remember seeing one down at Mr. Comby's barbershop, except for
Uncle Joe, Aunt Marguerite's husband, who is a Hill and is
half white. He and my father would hang out on the edges of
Coleman family gatherings, woofing on events and persons in
a barely audible stage whisper, like a two-person Greek
chorus. "Looks like the mourners' pew at a country funeral,"
I heard one of them say to the other at a reunion. And as soon
as I looked over at "the boys," sitting somberly in a row at the
picnic table, I busted out laughing. These guys could rain on
any parade when they got together. It was a major preoccupation of theirs, sitting around rattling ice in tall plastic cups of
iced tea, like blackbirds in a rhythm band, Daddy would say.
They had a weighty sense of family and tradition. Almost all
of them became born-again Christians near the end, like Big
Mom's brother, Uncle Boke, just before he went crazy.

Big Mom took Boke's death kind of hard. He was her younger brother. Otis Howard his proper name was, rhiney-colored leader of the Colored Prayer Band, head deacon and agent of the Holy Ghost, keeping watch for the Return of the Lord Himself. *Jee-zuhs.*

We had been playing on the playground, toward the middle of Erin Street. Aunt Ruth sold lemonade to the kids, and a water fountain did for our thirst what her lemonade couldn't do. The playground had monkey bars and a sliding board that must have been twenty feet tall, a basketball hoop and a baseball field and plenty of places to bike. I was on the monkey bars, sitting up there just swinging my legs, with a straight-ahead view of Uncle Boke's front door. He began running out with his hands in the air, imploring the Lord to take him now. He'd run outside to the middle of the road, shout and pray, and then he'd run back in. Three hours later, the message changed: The world was ending that day.

We thought it was funny, of course, and embarrassing. But as his behavior continued, it became scary, then sad. By nightfall, they had come to get him, hauling him off to Lakin, the colored insane asylum. Shoot me first, was all Daddy said, except to add that Boke had *always* been crazy, citing the night he had waited six hours in the rain at the bus stop at the bottom of Big Mom's hill for a phantom woman to return on a phantom bus. You see, one day Boke announced that Theresa Price, a black woman who was much younger than he was, was coming on the bus to meet him at the bus stop at the bottom of the hill in Piedmont. She never came; she was never going to. He had fantasized it all, in an earlier phase of his madness. He just stood there for hours in the rain, meeting all the buses. Had his good umbrella there too, Daddy pointed out, so she wouldn't be getting wet. Wonder what would have happened, he sometimes asks, if she actually showed up on that bus?

The thing about them niggers, Daddy says about his in-laws

with grudging admiration, was that they wanted to be self-sufficient. They'd drive fifty miles to save fifty cents, but they were ambitious and knew how to do things. Daddy meant that they were good with their hands. Carpentry, masonry, gardening, hunting, fishing. Just fixing things in general. If you can hammer it or oil it up, dem coons can do it.

The nine Coleman boys, with birth dates ranging from 1915 to 1933, were the last generation in our family conceived, born, and bred under segregation. Cradle-to-grave segregation. They were poor but talented and motivated. And they had to learn to stitch with the odds and ends left over from the bolts of whole cloth sitting on top of the tailor's table. Piecework. Colored piecework. Born barely working class—clawing and scraping your way out of starvation class, Daddy says—they carved out a dark-chocolate world, a world as nurturing as the loamy soil in Nemo's garden down at the bottom of Rat Tail Road. The tangle of family ties served as the netting that covered the garden's yield, setting it off from the chaos of flora that nature threw up in its undifferentiated madness of creation. That netting kept out predators, like birds and insects, who would wreak havoc on the order that weeks and months of after-hours labor had created. They would mouth the white man's commands in the day, to paraphrase Hurston, and enact their own legislation and jurisprudence in their sepia world at night.

The soul of that world was colored. Its inhabitants went to colored schools, they went to colored churches, they lived in colored neighborhoods, they ate colored food, they listened to colored music, and when all that fat and grease finally closed down their arteries or made their hearts explode, they slept in colored cemeteries, escorted there by colored preachers: old black-suited Southern preachers, with shiny black foreheads and an insatiable desire for fried chicken, men for whom preaching is a personal call from God, a direct line on His celestial cellular phone. They dated colored, married colored, divorced and cheated on colored. And when they could, they taught at colored colleges, preached to colored congregations, trimmed colored hair on nappy heads, and, after the fifties, even fought to keep alive the tradition of the segregated all-colored schools. They feared that world where so much humiliation had lain in wait, ambushing them blindsided, unawares. And they hated that which made them fear. That is, I think, why they hated some of us, the first generation of integrated wannabes, recognizing us as the real threat to the ordered universe they had constructed with such painstaking care for such a long time. It was like hoeing an acre of drought-stricken land with a wooden stick, Uncle Jim told me one day, out in the fishing boat, referring to their efforts to purchase the houses where they now lived.

Take the family reunions. The Coleman Family Reunion was inaugurated in 1949, the year before I was born. Nemo would ask permission of Mr. Baines or Mr. Bonner to use an acre of his farm, one that bordered Patterson's Creek or the South Branch of the Potomac. And we'd all gather there on the last Sunday in July, lounging on blankets that covered any overlooked cow pies, feasting off makeshift dining tables assembled for the occasion out of no. 2 pine two-by-fours. We'd play softball and badminton all day, swimming in between to cool ourselves off or to digest the feast of wonders that "the women" had prepared—from Aunt Marguerite's potato salad and Aunt Dot's fried chicken to Aunt Mary Jane's homemade cranberry sauce and Dorothy Ann's German chocolate cake, all washed down with Nemo's famous homemade root beer. Raymond took great pride in slicing the watermelon at the end of the day, the very last thing you did before cleaning up and stowing everything away in the trunks of the cars, to start the long journey back home to Piedmont, a world distant and all of ten or fifteen miles away.

Eventually they'd persuaded a real estate agent to part with an acre in a new development on the South Branch, then built the Coleman summer house, brick by brick, nail by nail, with their own hands, getting Teddy Twyman, the colored electrician up at the paper mill, to help with the wiring. In a hundred-acre field of trailers and Winnebagos, the Coleman boys had constructed a five-room house, complete with fireplace and picture window, a shower and a screened-in-porch and, a hundred feet away, a pavilion covering a table large enough to seat us all. And they did this before any of the rednecks who would be our neighbors could murmur any protest or raise even the barest hum of a fuss. Soon, in imitation, *they* started trying to turn their trailers into homes, structures with porches and cement foundations, just to keep up with the colored. Too late to burn the house down. Besides, hill folk generally didn't do that kind of thing. As long as there was only one colored in the field, things would be all right. Planted sod, too, and kept it neat. Showplace, the hill folk called it. A colored showplace.

6 / Down
to Cumberland

Because I lived in Piedmont, surrounded by my mother's brothers and sisters and dozens of their children, the Coleman family was familiar to me—all too familiar sometimes. And a contemptuous familiarity obtained between a few of Mama's brothers and me. The Gateses, on the other hand, lived in the mysterious world of Cumberland, Maryland, twenty-five miles, half a dozen shades of brown complexion, and as many grades of hair away. The rooms of their house had a certain worn and aging depth and the sort of dust-covered calm that suggested tradition. They drank beer and Scotch, played cards, read detective novels and traded them with each other, did crossword puzzles, and loved puns. Their favorite term of endearment was "Dummy."

The Colemans, by contrast, were the force of self-righteousness, teetotalers, non-smoking, non-gambling souls, who seemed to equate close-cropped, well-oiled hair and well-washed automobiles with the very purpose of life itself. One quickly realized that what one could or could not do "in front of Big Mom" was the ultimate mechanism for controlling the independent and the unruly.

Though I'd see my Coleman uncles, aunts, and cousins all together at our annual family reunions and Up the Hill at Big Mom's house on Christmas, I saw the Gateses all together on only two occasions in my childhood, and those were my grandparents' funerals.

I used to collect old photographs and paste them into albums. It was my first hobby; taking pictures was my second. I learned much of my family history, and especially the history of the Gateses, from old photographs. Daddy loved telling stories about his family, and I loved listening to them, mostly because they were so funny. The day that the photographs first came to life was the day of my grandfather's funeral.

Gateses never had family reunions and seemed to pride themselves on that fact. But funerals served the same function. I was ten when Pop Gates died. Standing next to my dad, I misread his silent sobs, his quivering shoulders. I thought Daddy was *laughing* right there in front of the casket, right there in front of everybody. His pop *did* look funny, laid out as he was, white as the driven snow. Maybe he *was* white, I remember thinking.

Funny as my grandfather looked lying in the casket, I was glad that somebody had the good sense to laugh. Maybe that would loosen things up a little in that funeral home, what with Aunt Helen crying like crazy. So I started to giggle and looked up into Daddy's face, his eyes red and glassy with tears, as he broke down and sobbed real loud. My mouth flew open, and I squeezed his hand. He had been crying! I started to cry too. I was holding the hand of a man I didn't even know. And for the first time in my life, I felt sorry for him.

Years later, when Mama died, Daddy told me how proud he was of Maggie and Liza, crying at the funeral. He likes his emotions *signed*. I didn't even notice, to tell you the truth. I wanted to be the child that day.

We were laughing, Liza confessed much later that day. We

didn't know *what* was going on, she said—we hardly knew Grams. When you all started crying we had started to laugh. Then we got scared and began to cry.

The crying was what Daddy saw. He appreciated it, was what he'd said. But of course I flashed back to old Pop Gates's funeral when I was ten and had done the same thing.

Pop Gates's funeral was the occasion at which I met my great-aunts, Pop's three sisters, Pansy, Lettitia, and Maude, their husbands—a dentist, a pharmacist, and a painter—and some of their children. That was also the day I realized that death could be big business, because each one had brought along a lawyer or a lawyer's opinion about Pop's will, and each of the three sisters sat occupying a corner of the living room, like battlements armed and well prepared to sustain a war. Only my dad seemed able to move from fort to castle to fort, like a neutral scout or the Secretary-General of the United Nations, trying to stall or prevent the outbreak of war.

That day was a revelation. Doctors and dentists, lawyers and pharmacists; Howard and Talladega, Harvard and Radcliffe—all of these careers and all of these schools were in my grandparents' living room that day, and each had a Gates face attached to it. It came as a shock to realize that these mythic characters in Daddy's tales were actual brown and tan and beige people. And refined. And well spoken. Obviously comfortable in the world. And they seemed to love my father's boys and seemed eager to hear tales of conquests ending with "straight A's." Yes, ma'am, a doctor, I said a hundred times. Maybe a brain surgeon. I'd seen that on *Ben Casey*.

They wanted a chunk of the property, just their rightful share, mind you, plus a share of all that cash Pop Gates used to stash in his secret hiding place on, or around, or under, the porch. Not one penny more. I bet them niggers will be bumping into each other on Pop's back porch tonight in the dark, Daddy had said, laughing, in the car as we drove past the still segregated Barton's Dairy Restaurant on the road back to Piedmont. Tearing up the bricks, looking for Pop's money. But nobody ever claimed to have found it.

Pop Gates had been left the property and everything else when his parents died. He had been the only one who had stayed behind to work the farm and then to establish several businesses with his father. They prospered, too: as chimney stokers who would light up your furnaces just before dawn and haul away the ashes as chimney sweeps; a cleaning service with lots of workers, who tended the businesses on Main Street. A bit of this, a bit of that. Good returns on the sale of some of the property that Old Man Brady left to Jane Gates, the first and oldest Gates, a slave. They had done all right. Everything paid for, every deed unencumbered. Never use credit, Pop had told my daddy for as long as he could remember.

In the midst of all the family grief, I went down with Daddy to help clear out his father's belongings. His mother, Nan— a wispy woman with a wicked wit—was in a fragile state, so we were all helping out. My grandfather kept lots and lots of scrapbooks, full of photographs and clippings and all sorts of memorabilia. Because they never had to move after 1882, they never threw anything away. They lived in a colored museum. Pop Gates also kept the family Bible, in the family for over a century, easy. Turning through the pages of the scrapbooks, past all sorts of clippings about Pop Gates's prized tulips and roses and the red and blue ribbons he had received for his tulips (his backyard looked like a botanical garden in summer, especially around the little rectangular goldfish pond banked with stone), we came across an obituary dated 1892. Its headline read as follows: DIED TODAY, JANE GATES, CITY. AN ESTIMABLE COLORED LADY. It was like stumbling onto the Rosetta Stone or Schliemann's uncovering Troy.

Jane Gates, as I've said, was the oldest Gates, our missing

link with Africa. We don't really know where in Africa she came from. But we do have a picture of her, a solid, brown-skinned woman with a midwife's cap on her head. That she was born in 1816 we know from the family Bible and from the obituary Daddy and I found.

In Pop's old trunk, we also found sepia photographs of all of Jane's children. Tall and thin, high cheekbones and light-yellow and cream colors, thin lips and "good hair." All of Jane's children were apparently fathered by one white man, the man who we think owned her. Supposedly his name was Brady, and he was an Irish property-owner who lived in Creasaptown, Maryland, just outside Cumberland. Jane's oldest son, Edward, was my great-grandfather. In his picture, he looked like a white man just as his son, Pop Gates, did. Maybe Brady loved her; maybe he just felt guilty; but sometime between the 1860 and 1870 censuses, Brady gave Jane a whole lot of land in western Maryland. Good land, too. The farm at Patterson's Creek has two hundred of the most beautiful acres of bottomland you'll ever see. That's where Gates Point is, the highest site in Mineral County. Patterson's Creek, an offshoot of the South Branch of the Potomac River, runs right through the property, full of trout and bass. The bottomland is surrounded by hills and mountains, abounding with wild turkey and deer, squirrels and rabbits.

A white family bought the farm in the twenties when the Gateses moved into their city house, which they had bought in 1882. There were no pictures of the farm, but there were numerous photographs of a handsome woman dressed in white, standing outside a wooden gazebo, and I wondered who she might be.

That was Pop Gates's mother, my great-grandmother, a matriarchal terror, by everyone's account. She was a bitch, Daddy said coldly, peering down at her photo. Her name was Maude Fortune, and where she came from is anybody's guess.

She loved to read, and she worshiped education. Sometime at the turn of the century, when Pop Gates was twenty-one, she decided to send her three daughters to Washington to get a formal education; she kept the boy at home to run the farm. He never forgave her or his three sisters (which is why they all brought lawyers to their brother's funeral). Two went to Howard, the other to Morgan. Two became teachers, the other a nurse. Daddy's grandma read the newspaper to her husband out loud each night, and together as a family they listened to the news on the radio. He read only with difficulty; when she got cataracts, they were forced to switch roles, with him reading to her out loud at night. That was hell on everybody, Daddy says. She loved Germans and German culture, and nicknamed Daddy "Heinie," when he was born in 1913, despite the fact that a world war was looming, and Germany would be fighting on the other side. She became a socialist in 1919 and was the first colored person in Cumberland to subscribe to W. E. B. Du Bois's *Crisis* magazine. She died a socialist. Her husband was a Lincoln Republican.

In 1890, Maude Gates founded St. Phillips Episcopal Church in Cumberland; colored priests from Haiti and Jamaica were enlisted to serve there. Maude's daughters' children did well: They all graduated from college, from Howard to Harvard. Three generations at Howard, including the board of trustees, two generations at Harvard, including Harvard Law School. Three generations of dentists and three of doctors. On her son's side, however, the story is a different one. His seven sons all went to work at factories, although my daddy attended school in New Jersey for a while. That was around the time that he had wanted to be a priest. He was the head acolyte within his generation, the seventh son, the golden boy on whose head grew Jesus Moss. His aunt Pansy, who told me she had wanted to adopt him, had sent him up to Newark, New Jersey, where he attended a predominantly

Jewish school. Everyone there thought he was Jewish, until he went to school on Rosh Hashanah. "Heinie," his teacher asked him, "what are you doing in school today? It's Rosh Hashanah." "Rosh what?" Daddy replied. His uncle Fred had passed for Jewish, had even married a Jewish woman. He never contacted the family again. When Maude, his mother, died, Pop Gates refused to contact him, his own brother. Passing is not regarded with great favor in our family.

Which may seem curious since, until a generation ago, most of the Gateses qualified as octoroons—"light and bright and damn near white," Daddy said, turning the pages of the photo album. My grandfather and his father looked like white people, and they married the lightest black people they could find. Shit-colored niggers with Jesus Moss, people used to say. No need to claim they were part Irish, part English, part Dutch, part German, part anything, as my Coleman cousins and I felt compelled to do when we were around white kids in school. No, these people wore the complexity of their bloodlines on their faces and on the crowns of their heads.

One day, Pop Gates had called Aunt Helen into the parlor and told her to take a bag of money over to Cumberland's main bank. Ask for Mr. Brady, he stressed. When she came home and handed him the receipt, he asked what Mr. Brady had said to her. He didn't say anything, she said, not after he asked me if I was a Gates. He just stared at me in a funny way.

He's your cousin, was all Pop Gates had said, and you remind him of his sister.

My father's generation, sensing a depletion of the gene pool, so it's been said, married the darkest Negroes they could find. Except for one brother, who liked white women and went crazy one day after he fell in love with the sales clerk in the Cumberland jewelry store where he worked in the back. So crazy he pulled a gun on his beloved's husband and ordered him to stay away from her, she was his woman now . . . then was taken straight to jail. A few of his brothers bailed him out. I remember the day that Daddy got his call from prison. Got to go and bail out my brother, he said, pushing his chair back from the kitchen table. Running that white woman again.

It was a day trip to visit Daddy's family, down to Cumberland. Daddy never learned to drive, so about once a month, on his day off, he, my brother Rocky, and I would take the yellow-and-orange Osgood bus from East Hampshire Street to Cumberland. We'd play "reading the signs" or "spotting the horses," and the person who saw the most horses won the prize that day. Learning how to spot phantom horses that nobody else could see was part of the art of the game, and the fun, especially if you could do it artfully.

We'd get off at Greene Street in Cumberland and begin the rounds, house-hopping from one of Daddy's brothers to the next, starting with Nan's and Pop's house and ending up at Aunt Helen's and Uncle Bill's, before dropping in briefly to say goodbye to Nan again, since her house was closest to the bus stop. At lunchtime, we'd go downtown and across the tracks to Hammersmith's, a dark beer joint with a colored section, which served the best fried-fish sandwiches and french fries in the world. Daddy would drink a beer and spend a lot of time talking to his old buddies from Carver High School, the guys he used to be wild and crazy with. He'd tell the funniest stories about getting in trouble. He was *always* in some kind of trouble.

"I just didn't give a damn," he'd say. I don't think this was strictly true. But he was in trouble a lot, skipping school and playing hooky, and he loved to drink and to gamble.

A milk truck ran over his foot once when he was a boy, sitting on a curb watching the new electric scoreboard in downtown Cumberland. Pop Gates's brother, Great-uncle Guy, a doctor in Washington, came up to Cumberland for the weekend. He unwrapped Daddy's foot slowly and carefully, took a good look at it, then said, "It's broken, all right," and proceeded to wrap it up again. Daddy says he thought that was funny even then, unlike all sorts of things that are funny only years later, when the pain stops hurting. They got five hundred dollars as settlement, which his father promptly borrowed to buy a new Ford Model T.

Years later, when he was dying, Pop Gates confessed how guilty he'd felt for not returning that money. All that time feeling guilty for taking settlement money from a twelve-year-old's smashed foot, which probably shouldn't have been on the road in the first place.

Daddy was particularly close to his sister Helen. Helen and he argued constantly, laughing and joking all the way. One of their recurrent topics of conversation was a bet they once had, which Daddy apparently lost, giving Aunt Helen an IOU. Daddy said that Helen was "old and dotty," that he hadn't lost that bet at all, and even if he had, where was the proof? Show me the piece of paper. No IOU, no money. Helen would busy herself calculating the compound interest on a twenty-five-cent bet over a thirty-year period. Compounded *daily*. I'm a millionaire, she'd tell him, as long as you owe me. Years later, Helen found the Gates family Bible, which was falling apart, and she hauled it out to see if I knew how to get it fixed. I'd be happy to get it rebound, I said. As we leafed through its pages, yellowing and fragile, out fell a faded sheet of notepaper, which to everyone's astonishment read: "I.O.U. 25 cents. Signed, Heinie Gates, July 25, 1925." Daddy snatched that piece of paper and—it still pains me to relate—ripped it to shreds.

When I was going on fifteen, I had taken off school to attend the funeral of Daddy's favorite niece, Carolyn. She had been very beautiful and was just ten years older than I was. Though usually the funerals of the Gateses are reunions or parties, with cousins meeting cousins and everybody drinking and telling lies, being extra funny to heal the sadness, nobody did any of those things this time. Everyone was just sad and spent a lot of time crying, and whispering in corners.

Carolyn had left three small children, two girls and a boy, and a huge custody battle was about to erupt between her sister, Jane, and her jive-time husband, Ernie. That is the lyingest nigger on earth, Uncle Bill had said. He did lie a lot. There was the time that he unveiled all the trophies he had won in his hometown in Ohio, where he had been a great athlete. How impressed everybody had been—until the man who owned the local trophy store asked Uncle Bob just what Ernie was going to do with all those awards he had bought.

No one seemed to know what Carolyn died of. I heard about a brain tumor, then some sort of fever, then this, then that. People lied so much about it that they forgot which disease they had used the last time they discussed it. So finally, a week or so later, I asked Daddy what the truth was. He wasn't sure, he said, but one story was that she had been mutilated in an illegal abortion and had bled to death. At the age of twenty-five.

Since the festive air that typified the Gates funerals I had attended was absent at hers, I could take my time and look around the cemetery. It was a graveyard full of Gateses, going back well over a hundred years. We were all buried there, under worn flat markers in the nineteenth century, medium-size headstones later on. Even babies were there, like Daddy's seventh brother, Charles. I felt cloaked in the mantle of my family at that cemetery.

As I grew up, the family farm at Patterson's Creek in West Virginia gained in significance for me. Despite the fact that we no longer owned it, I visited it several times in my teens. Daddy and I used to walk all over it, reliving scenes from his memory. Things he had been telling my brother and me for years were brought to life here in the place where they had occurred. Like the cave we stumbled on, which, when we were kids, Daddy would say was full of gold coins. Whenever I heard "Ali Baba and the Forty Thieves," I'd think about our cave, and wonder if I'd stumble upon equally magic words. Daddy had shown me the very gate to the property where his father had bumped into Helen Redman one day, decided that she looked just like a little china doll, and begun to court her. The barn where Pop Gates's horse, Old Toag, had been hitched to the buggy still stood.

It was in the living room, with its stone fireplace, that Dr. Rayford Logan had shown up one day from Washington to ask for Lettitia Gates's hand. Logan, who took the Ph.D. in history from Harvard, was a *gentleman*, Grandma declared. He was drafted during the war, went off to France in 1917, and decided to stay in Paris, where he felt free and a man. So Lettitia married Russell Carpenter instead. He used to call everybody "Chappy." Carpenter left Lettitia at the age of sixty-five and married a white woman who looked just like her. Like an old witch, Daddy would say. In the late 1970s, I met Rayford Logan, then a renowned historian, when we brought him to Yale to deliver an endowed lecture. He seemed astounded that I was Lettitia's descendant; he begged me for tales about her and asked me for her picture. His eyes said that he thought he'd stayed in Paris a bit too long.

7 / Playing Hardball

Daddy worked all the time, every day but Sunday. Two jobs—twice a day, in and out, eat and work, work and eat. Evenings, we watched television together, all of us, after I'd done my homework and Daddy had devoured the newspaper or a book. He was always reading, it seemed, especially detective stories. He was a charter subscriber to *Alfred Hitchcock's Magazine* and loved detective movies on TV.

My brother Rocky was the one he was close to. Rocky worshiped sports, while I worshiped Rocky. I chased after him like a lapdog. I wanted to be just like him. But the five years between us loomed like Kilimanjaro. We were always out of phase. And he felt crowded by my adoring gaze.

Rocky and I didn't exactly start off on the right foot. When I was born, my parents moved my brother to Big Mom's house, to live with her and Little Jim, who was our first cousin and Nemo's son and the firstborn male of our generation in the Coleman family. It was not an uncommon arrangement to shift an older child to his or her grandparents', because of crowding. Since we had only three rooms, plus a tiny room with a toilet, my parents thought the move was for the best. And Big Mom's house was only a couple hundred yards straight up the hill. Still, it's difficult to gauge the trauma of that displacement, all these years later. Five years of bliss, ended by my big head popping out.

But Rocky was compensated: he was Daddy's boy. Like the rest of Piedmont, they were baseball fanatics. They knew who had done what and when, how much everyone had hit, in what inning, who had scored the most runs in 1922, who the most rbi's. They could sit in front of a TV for hours at a time, watching inning after tedious inning of baseball, baseball, baseball. Or sit at Forbes Field in Pittsburgh through a doubleheader without getting tired or longing to go home. One night, when I was seven, we saw Sandy Koufax of the Dodgers pitch one game, then his teammate Don Drysdale pitch another. It was the most boring night of my life, though later I came to realize what a feat I had witnessed, two of baseball's greatest pitchers back-to-back.

I enjoyed *going* to the games in Pittsburgh because even then I loved to travel. One of Daddy's friends would drive me. I was fascinated with geography. And since I was even more fascinated with food, a keen and abiding interest of mine, I liked the games for that reason too. We would stop to eat at Howard Johnson's, going and coming. And there'd be hot dogs and sodas at the games, as well as popcorn and candy, to pass the eternity of successive innings in the July heat. Howard Johnson's was a five-star restaurant in Piedmont.

I used to get up early to have breakfast with Daddy, eating from his plate. I'll still spear a heavily peppered fried potato or a bit of egg off his plate today. My food didn't taste as good as his. Still doesn't. I used to drink coffee, too, in order to be just like Daddy. "Coffee will make you black," he'd tell me, with the intention of putting me off. From the beginning, I used a lot of pepper, because he did, and he did because his father did. I remember reading James Agee's *A Death in the Family* and being moved by a description of the extra pepper that the father's wife put on his eggs the very morning that he is killed in a car. Why are you frying eggs *this* time of day, Mama asked me that evening. Have you seen the pepper, Mama? I replied.

An unathletic child with too great an interest in food—no wonder I was fat, and therefore compelled to wear "husky" clothes.

My Skippy's not *fat*, Mama would lie. He's husky.

But I *was* fat, and felt fatter every time Mama repeated her lie. My mama loved me like life itself. Maybe she didn't see me as fat. But I was. And whoever thought of the euphemism "husky" should be shot. I was short and round—not obese, mind you, but *fat*. Still, I was clean and energetic, and most of the time I was cheerful. And I liked to play with other kids, not so much because I enjoyed the things we did together but because I could watch them be happy.

But sports created a bond between Rocky and my father that excluded me, and, though my father had no known athletic talent himself, my own unathletic bearing compounded my problems. For not only was I overweight; I had been born with flat feet and wore "corrective shoes." They were the bane of my existence, those shoes. While Rocky would be wearing long, pointy-toed, cool leather gentlemen, I'd be shod in blunt-ended, round-toed, fat-footed shoes that nobody but your mother could love.

And Mama *did* love those shoes. Elegant, she'd say. They're Stride-Rite. Stride-wrong, I'd think. Mama, I want some nice shoes, I'd beg, like Rocky's.

Still, I guess they did what they were meant to do, because I have good arches now. Even today, I look at the imprint of my wet foot at a swimming pool, just to make certain that my arch is still arched. I don't ever again want to wear those dull brown or black corrective shoes.

What made it all the more poignant was that Rocky—tall, lean, and handsome, blessed with my father's metabolism—was a true athlete. He would be the first Negro captain of the basketball team in high school and receive "the watch" at graduation. (He was the first colored to do that too.)

Maybe Mama thought I was husky, but Daddy knew better, and he made no secret of it. "Two-Ton Tony Galento," he and Rocky would say, or they'd call me Chicken Flinsterwall or Fletcher Bissett, Milton Berle's or Jack Benny's character in a made-for-TV movie about two complete cowards. I hated Daddy for doing that and yielded him as unconquerable terrain to my brother, clinging desperately to my mother for protection.

Ironically, I had Daddy's athletic ability, or lack thereof, just as I have his body. (We wear the same-size ring, gloves, shoes, shirt, suits, and hat.) And like him, I love to hear a good story. But during my first twelve or so years we were alienated from each other. I despised sports because I was overweight and scared to death. Especially of baseball—hardball, we called it. Yet I felt I had no choice but to try out for Little League. Everyone my age did Little League, after all. They made me a Giant, decided I was a catcher because I was "stout, like Roy Campanella," dressed me in a chest protector and a mask, and squatted me behind a batter.

It's hard to catch a baseball with your eyes closed. Each time a ball came over the plate, I thanked the Good Lord that the batter hadn't confused my nappy head with the baseball that had popped its way into my mitt. My one time at bat was an experience in blindness; miraculously, I wasn't hit in the head. With a 3 and 2 count, I got a ball, so I walked. They put in a runner for me. Everybody patted me on the back like I had just won the World Series. And everybody said nice things about my "eye." Yeah, I thought. My tightly closed eye.

Afterward, Pop and I stopped at the Cut-Rate to get a caramel ice cream cone, then began the long walk up the hill to Pearl Street. I was exhausted, so we walked easy. He was biding his time, taking smaller steps than usual so that I could keep up. "You know that you don't have to play baseball, don't you, boy?" All of a sudden I knew how Moses had felt on Mount Sinai. His voice was a bolt out of the blue. Oh, I want to play, I responded in a squeaky voice. "But you know that you don't *have* to play. I never was a good player. Always afraid of the ball. Uncoordinated too. I can't even run straight." We laughed. "I became the manager of the team," he said. That caramel ice cream sure tasted good. I held Daddy's hand almost all the way home.

In my one time at bat, I had got on base. I had confronted the dragon and he was mine. I had, I had . . . been absurdly lucky . . . and I couldn't *wait* to give them back their baseball suit. It was about that time that Daddy stopped teasing me about being fat. That day he knew me, and he seemed to care.

Yes, Pop and I had some hard times. He thought that I didn't love him, and I thought he didn't love me. At times, we both were right. I didn't think you wanted me around, he told me much later. I thought that I embarrassed you. He did embarrass me, but not like you might think, not the usual way parents embarrass children in front of their friends, for example. He had a habit of correcting me in front of strangers or white people, especially if they were settling an argument between me and Pop by something they had just said, by a question they had answered. See, I *told* you so, he'd say loudly, embarrassing the hell out of me with a deliberateness that puzzled and vexed me. I hated him when he did that.

And despite my efforts to keep up, he and my brother had somehow made me feel as if I were an android, something not quite a person. I used to dream about going away to military school, and wrote to our Congressman, Harley Staggers, for a list of names. I used to devour *McKeever and the Colonel* on Sunday nights and dream about the freedom of starting over, at a high-powered, regimented school away from home. Daddy and Rocky would make heavy-handed jokes about queers and sissies. I wasn't their direct target, but I guess it was another form of masculine camaraderie that marked me as less manly than my brother.

And while I didn't fantasize about boys, I did love the companionship of boys and men, loved hearing them talk and watching their rituals, loved the warmth that their company could bring. I even loved being with the Coleman boys, at one of their shrimp or squirrel feeds, when they would play cards. Generally, though, I just enjoyed being on the edge of the circle, watching and listening and laughing, basking in the warmth, memorizing the stories, trying to strip away illusions, getting at what was really coming down.

I made my peace with sports, by and by, and was comfortable watching Rock and Daddy watch sports. But I could never experience it with the absorption they were capable of, could never live and breathe sports as they did. Oh, I loved to watch all the tournaments, the finals, the Olympics—the ritual events. But my relation to sports was never as visceral and direct as theirs.

After I returned my Little League uniform, I became the team's batboy and then the league's official scorekeeper, publishing our results in a column in the *Piedmont Herald*, our weekly newspaper.

Much more than for sports, I had early on developed an avidity for information about The Negro. I'm not sure why, since Daddy was not exactly a race man. Niggers are crabs in a barrel: if he said that once, he said it to us a thousand times. My father was hard on colored people—and funny about it too.

Aside from the brief stint as a student in New Jersey, Daddy's major contact with Negro culture from Elsewhere had been in the army, at Camp Lee, Virginia. He used to tell us all kinds of stories about the colored troops at Camp Lee, especially blacks from the rural South. It was clear that the army in World War II had been a great cauldron, mixing the New Negro culture, which had developed in the cities since the great migration of the twenties and thirties, and the Old Negro culture, the remnants of traditional rural black culture in the South.

Camp Lee was where colored soldiers were sent to learn how to be quartermasters—butlers, chefs, and service people, generally. Because the Army replicates the social structure of the larger society it defends, almost all black draftees were taught to cook and clean. Of course, it was usually women who cooked and cleaned outside the Army, but *someone* had to do the work, so it would be black men. Gender and race conflate in a crisis. Even educated black people were put in the quartermasters.

Well, Camp Lee was a circus and my daddy its scribe. He told us stories about how he beat the system, or damn well tried to. The first day, he had raised his hand when an officer asked who knew accounting. How hard could it be? he responded when I laughed. Hell, all you had to be able to do was add and subtract. The one thing I knew, he said, was that an accountant had an office and everybody else had to do basic training. Now, which one would *you* have picked? For two years, he stayed at Camp Lee and avoided being shipped to the front. Everybody else would be processed, then shipped out to Europe. But Daddy became a staff sergeant, serving as secretary and accountant to the commanding officer, who liked him a lot. He sent for Mama, who took a room in a colored home in town. Daddy slept there too. Mama got a job in a dry cleaners. The pictures that I carry of them in my wallet are from this time, 1942.

The war wouldn't take Pop any farther than Camp Lee, but

even that was an experience that stayed with him. There he encountered the customs and sayings, the myths and folklore, of all sorts of black people he had never even heard about. The war did more to recement black American culture, which migration had fragmented, than did any other single event or experience. "War? What is it good for? You tell 'em: absolutely nothing." Nothing for the Negro but the transfer of cultures, the merging of the old black cultures with the new. And the transfer of skills. Daddy was no "race man," but for all his sardonicism, he respected race men and women, the people who were articulate and well educated, who comported themselves with dignity and who "achieved." Being at Camp Lee, an all-colored world, he'd say a decade later, was like watching episodes of *Amos and Andy*.

Hard as Daddy could be on colored people, he was Marcus Garvey compared to *his* father. Pop Gates used to claim that the government should lock up all the niggers in a big reservation in Kansas or Oklahoma or somewhere, feed them, clothe them, and give them two names: John or Mary. Nobody would hurt them, he'd add plaintively when his children would either protest or burst into howls of laughter. Pop Gates *hated* to see black people in loud clothes, and he hated just as much our traditional poetic names, such as Arbadella or Ethelretta. Made-up names, he'd say. Shouldn't be allowed, he'd say.

I was more aggressive around white people than Daddy, and it didn't go down well with him—or anybody else. Especially my Coleman uncles. Daddy, as noted, would almost never take my side in front of others. And if he felt I had violated a boundary, he would name it publicly and side with the boundary. He would do so loudly, even with what struck my child's ears as a certain malice. It tore me up.

He was not always this way with me. At a Little League game when I was ten, I told off a white man, Mr. Frank Price, not for anything he'd done to me, but for the rude way he treated Mr. Stanley Fisher, a black man in his sixties, who was maybe twenty years Price's senior. The details are murky, but Price had been rude to the older man in a way that crossed a line, that made the colored people feel he was a racist.

I do remember that I was unable to control myself, unable to contain my anger. I found myself acting without thinking. I felt the blood rushing to my face, and a flood of nasty words poured out of my mouth, just this side of profanity. Everybody on the first-base side of the Little League field over in Westernport looked up and froze in silence as I stood in front of that big-bellied man's fat red face and told him to leave Mr. Stanley alone. Then I turned to Mr. Stanley and told him not to waste his dignity on that trash: "Don't sweat the small stuff," I said. The colored held their breaths, and Daddy looked like a cat caught between two fighting dogs and not knowing which way to turn. Even Mr. Stanley's face showed surprise at this snot-nosed kid talking right up in some redneck's face. Mr. Stanley must have been more embarrassed by me than reassured.

Daddy stepped in finally, put his arm around my shoulder, and started woofing at Frank Price and giving him those dirty glares of his, all the while pushing me gently up the field toward Stanley and the colored men who always sat together on their lawn chairs out in right field. And we then all walked together up the dusty back road that bordered the Little League field like the rim of a crater, passing the new filtration plant, which made the whole place stink worse than the sulfurous chemicals that it had been built to remove, and all the old colored men were saying what an asshole Frank Price was and always had been, and how he had been rude to Stanley, and how nobody liked or respected him (not even white people), and how nobody within earshot should pay that motherfucker no mind.

Now, you know you are supposed to respect your elders, don't you? Daddy said to me much later, after we had bought a caramel ice cream cone, to go, at the Cut-Rate. And you know you are not supposed to talk back to older people, now don't you? And you know that Stanley Fisher can take care of himself? And you know that you can get in trouble talking back to white people, don't you? Don't you, boy? Boy, you crazy sometimes. That ice cream is dripping down your fingers. Don't let it go to waste.

III / Over in the Orchard

8 / Current Events

L ess than four years after my birth, something happened
that would indelibly mark me and my peers for life—
something that would open up another world to us, a
world our parents could never have known. *Brown* v. *Board*
was decided in 1954.

I entered the Davis Free Elementary School in 1956, just
one year after it was integrated. There are many places where
the integration of the schools lagged behind that of other social
institutions. The opposite was true of Piedmont. What made
the Supreme Court decision so determining for us was that
school was for many years after 1955 virtually the only integrated arena in Piedmont.

To their credit, Mr. Harley Dixon and the other commis-
sioners of the county school board responded quickly to the
new judicial order. Otherwise it might have taken us a hundred more years to integrate, because everybody colored was
devoted to Howard High School. They liked the teachers,
they liked the principal, they liked the building and the basketball team. They liked its dignity and pride. They did not
like its worn-down textbooks, the ones sent up by the board

of education when the white schools got tired of them or when they were outdated. Other than that, Howard High was quite fine, thank you very much, your ticket to ride if you worked hard enough.

When I started at the white school in '56, everybody I knew was excited about integration, and everybody was scared. Mama would grill us every day about who said what and *how*. Mama did not play when it came to her boys, and she wasn't going to let any white woman or man step on her babies' dreams.

In the newly integrated school system, race was like an item of apparel that fitted us up all tight, like one of Mama's girdles or the garters that supported her hose. Nobody ever *talked* about race, but it was there in the lines drawn around socializing. Look, but don't touch. Don't even think about asking that white girl to dance. Obey that rule and everything will be fine. We'll all get along. Colored go with colored; white with white.

School—the elementary school at the top of Kenny House Hill and the high school over in the Orchard—was a fairly constant clash of cultures, especially for the older kids, who had had a segregated education all those years and had lived rigidly segregated lives for so very long. Cultural clashes, like the time that Mr. Staggers, the principal, asked Arthur Galloway what he had done to his hair, and Audie said he had gotten a process. And Mr. Staggers asked him what a process was. And Audie told him the truth, explaining about a mixture of mashed potatoes, eggs, and lye, and how you smear it on your hair with a paintbrush, and how it burns the kink right out. And Mr. Staggers interrupted Audie, accused him of lying, and took him to the office to impose corporal punishment on his behind with his favorite paddle, "Mr. Walnut,"

specially made with holes in it for improved aerodynamics.
Or the day that Mr. Staggers asked one of the colored kids if
he knew any poetry, and the fool said yes, "Shine and the
Titanic," and Mr. Staggers asked that he recite a verse or two,
only to halt the student, alarmed and panicked, when he got
to the part about Mrs. Astor raising her dress and offering to
trade sex for her survival. Daddy would say that people who
could barely remember their names could recite twenty verses
of "The Signifying Monkey" and "Shine and the Titanic":

> "Shine, Shine, save poor me—
> I'll make you as rich as a shine can be."
> And Shine said:
> Money's good but money don't last—
> Shine's gonna save his own black ass.
> And Shine swam on.

The two-week suspension was all anybody talked about down
at the colored Legion in Keyser.

By the time I showed up at the "white school" (as we still
thought of it), they were expecting me. Mama used to clean
the houses of my teachers, Mrs. Mellor and Mrs. Bell, and
they respected her. One time I referred to Mama as "she,"
and Mrs. Bell lectured me in front of the entire fourth-grade
class about referring to someone like my mother with a pro-
noun. Your mother is a lady, a real lady. What is wrong with
you? she asked. Have you bumped your head? It made me
feel good, this white woman talking about my mama like that,
in front of the other kids.

From the first day of first grade, I was marked out to excel.
My brother's performance had been outstanding the year before, and I had shone in the preschool test. I was quiet, I was
smart, I had a good memory, I already knew how to read and
write, and I was blessed with the belief that I could learn

anything. I was all set to become the little prince of that almost all-white school. The little brown prince with a stocking cap for a crown.

The teachers, in turn, pushed me and encouraged me. Except for Mrs. Sheetz, my first-grade teacher, who accused me of stealing her scissors. Why? Because I had laughed when, in her inquisition of the class, going down each row of desks, pupil to pupil, she finally got to me. I was so astonished at the idea that I laughed some more, which hung a cloud of accusation over my head until I got home with her note. Did you take her scissors? Mama asked. All I want to know, Daddy interrupted Mama, is, Did you take the scissors? Just tell us the truth and we're behind you. I laughed again, aching with the laughter. No, I don't have her scissors. Why would I do a thing like that? Bonnie Gilroy had the scissors; Bonnie Gilroy, the trashiest of the white trash, had had those scissors all along. She used to bring plastic bleach jugs up to our house, and we'd fill them with water for drinking. She was scrawny and scraggly, greasy, dirty, and dumb. I'd have looked at Bonnie first, had I been Mrs. Sheetz. After that I hated Mrs. Sheetz with all my injured pride and delighted in scoring all A's in her class for the rest of that first year.

By second grade, it was entirely my world; there wasn't anything I couldn't learn. I loved the way Mrs. Mellor said my name Louis, as I was called (thank God nobody used my middle name, Smith, which I hated and longed to change). They gave me a test in the middle of the year, and I got 489 answers right out of 500. The other teachers had come down to Mrs. Mellor's room at the end of the hall, to the right of the boys' bathroom, and stared at the score sheet she was holding and then at me. I took to wearing a white cotton boat-neck sweatshirt with a chessboard on its front, like a personal coat of arms. These teachers were serious about learning, and about school. Piedmont had turned out most of the county's doctors. In a school of six grades and only 250 or so kids, that is quite something.

If I was the school's prince, my princess was Linda Hoffman. It was inevitable. Linda and I were the best students in our class. Linda and I were soul mates, or so I fantasized. She ate books. She read more books more quickly and with greater comprehension than anybody I knew. Total concentration was her gift. We were an item: long, deep stares into her eyes, lots of times, every day. She called me Gates, just like Mama called Daddy, and I called her Hoffman, or Linda H. We exchanged pictures every year and gave each other an extra valentine in the brown-bag "mailboxes" we made for the occasion. The teachers often paired us together, because our combined magic was so powerful.

I revered Linda H. I used to walk half a mile out of my way just so I could pass her house and maybe catch a glimpse of her. One day when I was in fourth grade, a traveling magician came to town. The entire six grades assembled, to walk two abreast down Kenny House Hill, across the tracks, over to the Orchard, and past the pool to the high school, where special assemblies were held. At some point in his act, the magician asked for a student volunteer, and somehow he chose Hoffman.

Pick your little boyfriend, honey, he said. I want Skippy, was all I heard Linda say, before the whole auditorium erupted in surprise and nervous laughter. I felt chagrined and maybe a little proud as I joined her on the stage.

Well, that didn't play. In that school, no white girl and colored boy had yet stood onstage together. I thought that Mr. Magician would do his World-Famous Disappearing Act. He managed to do his trick, whatever it was, but it was clear that he was flustered, and he shooed us off as soon as he could. Thank God he hadn't tried to make my hair stand on end with a static-electricity machine.

"I want Skippy, I want Skippy"—that's all I heard from the older colored kids, over and over again. Interracial dating was taboo in Piedmont. Like Booker T. Washington had said in 1895 in Atlanta, in all things educational we were as one, like a clenched fist, but in all things social we were the five separate fingers. Colored danced with colored, white danced with white. At the operettas and the Junior Fair, they'd make two colored boys or two white boys or girls dance together, if the numbers of boys to girls was uneven. Or a colored boy and a white boy, if that was absolutely essential to the artistic success of our rinky-dink productions. But never cross the line of race *and* gender. You couldn't even think about that.

Which is probably why we thought about it all the time.

But things could be no other way. The school board had worked out all sorts of compromises to enable integration in the county to proceed. No dating, of course, no holding hands, no dancing. Not too many colored on the starting lineup of the basketball teams. One colored cheerleader, max. Hire one colored elementary teacher, one in the high school (make that one the former principal of the colored school). Put most of the colored in the B track, vocational, but treat the A group fairly. Corporal punishment to be meted out for racial infractions. Give regular lectures on hygiene. Don't rock the social boat. You'll get along as long as you abide by the rules.

Rocky's friends and my friends—the ones we invited to our home, I mean—were all colored. My friend Rodney would stay over a lot. So would Jerry and Roland. But I didn't have overnight white friends, ever. In eighteen years of living in Piedmont, going to school with white kids for twelve, I never had a single white friend over for dinner. Nor would anyone white have ever invited me. And I had some good white friends, too. Like Johnny DiPilato.

I went to Johnny's house several times, but only for a hot minute or two. Like I said, I never got invited for dinner. Yet his mom was very nice to me, genuinely nice, not with one of those tight smiles that say: What are you doing in my house, you little nigger boy, and how soon are you going to get your little colored ass offa my sofa? She called Mama Mrs. Gates, and Mama called her Mrs. DiPilato. That was rare in Piedmont. Colored people might call each other Miss, Mrs., or Mr., to show respect. But colored people continued to call white people Miss or Mrs. or Mr. even when those white people addressed them by their Christian names. I guess Johnny Dip was always slightly off-center because his father had a thick Italian accent, which was easily imitated. Skeep, he'd call me. Johnny was ashamed of his father's accent. You could see it in his face and in the way he'd defy his father and say rude things right in front of him.

I used to go over to Pat Amoroso's house in the Orchard and sit in his kitchen or on his steps, but only if his father was asleep or wasn't home. His father hated niggers. It was as simple as that. Nobody colored much minded. He had a right, people said. I'd hate niggers, too, if . . . That's how people would explain him away. What he really hated was the fact that his son, Donny, had been killed late one night in a hit-and-run accident right at the crest of old Snaky. And Gerry Washington had been driving. Driving drunk, on the wrong side of the road, up over the hill. Then he had run down the tracks to hide, before they caught his black ass. So instead of mourning like a normal person, Mr. Amoroso decided to hate niggers. It was his way of bearing witness, of remembering his son, of showing his love and his grief. Actually, he could be pretty nice when he forgot you were a nigger. We all felt sorry for Mr. Amoroso. We all understood. Two years ago, Gerry Washington got killed in a car in D.C. or somewhere. "Just like he killed that Amoroso boy," the town said. Everybody understood why he had to die like he did.

An eye for an eye is a major precept in Piedmont, though most people prefer retributive woofing to retributive justice. *Somethin' bad gonna happen to that nigger, and God don't like ugly.*

One factor that eased my passage in school was the fact that Rocky was the pioneer, so he got the brunt of the problems that lay in wait. There was the time when Mrs. Bright told Rocky that he didn't need coaching for the literary competition, he was already perfect, so Mama coached him every night till he got James Weldon Johnson's great poem, "The Creation," right. Rocky stepped out on that stage and, with the power and force of Mama's coaching, blew the Drane girl to Timbuktu. Mrs. Bright almost fainted because she had wanted that Drane girl to demolish my brother.

It was Mama who took the battle to them, Mama who showed us how to fight. We didn't always win, of course. In eighth grade, Rocky couldn't be awarded West Virginia's most coveted prize for excellence in state history, a Golden Horseshoe, one of Daddy's white friends told us, because the hotel where we would have had to stay in the state capital was segregated. Hell, they'd just denied entry to Elgin Baylor, the star forward of the Minneapolis Lakers. Rocky had missed winning by "half a point," they said. He had misspelled a word, they said. Too bad, they said. Sometimes it seems Rocky's childhood ended that day, the day he found out why he had not won. Now, a Golden Horseshoe is the Nobel Prize of eighth graders in West Virginia. Your entire education has prepared you for this competition. Four winners per county. Meeting the governor. Fame. Glory.

One half point. A misspelled word. How it haunted Rocky! Then Elmer Shaver—the white man who was Daddy's boss at the phone company and one of his best friends—came up one night, late, and explained the whole thing in a whispered voice, while Rocky and I sat on our bunks in our bedroom, listening to John R. out of *Randy's Record Shop* in Gallatin, Tennessee. And then, after Mr. Shaver left, Mama tried to find the voice to tell it, to tell the awful truth of what those crackers did. How relieved Rocky was that it was not his fault, that he had not blown the chance of a lifetime to be the first colored Golden Horseshoe winner by transposing some letters.

But then, as soon as you let yourself feel relief, this next wave came crashing over you, larger and more dangerous than the first wave, of guilt and responsibility, and this wave was the terrible one, this wave crushing and inexorable: no matter what you did or how you did it, it didn't matter because it was their world, their sea, and their tide, and your little black ass was about as significant as a grain of yellow sand.

Something died inside, the part that spells the difference between hoping and doing, between casting wide or casting close, between wearing the horizon like a shawl around your shoulders or allowing it to choke you to death like one of those plastic dry cleaner's bags that warn of suffocation in dire blue letters. And something happened to Rocky when that county school board lied and told him that he had almost won, that he should have worked just a little harder, that he transposed two letters. That it could have happened to anyone, boy—but especially to you, *boy*.

I saw him nursing the injury in silence, unable to speak of it, unwilling to shed it. Paltry as it may seem from the vantage of adulthood, the knowledge of that deception cast a shadow over his life. That same knowledge drove me to win a Golden Horseshoe six years later.

Rocky kept tripping over those rules that you didn't know existed until you broke them. Like being selected in the eleventh grade by the school for Boys State, whereupon the white

American Legion, led by Frank Price, informed the board
that they preferred a white boy. Mr. Staggers, the principal,
had to inform Frank Price that they'd take Paul Gates or send
no one at all. He went, and we all rejoiced at another victory
for the Negro race. But Rocky hurt from this sort of thing.

Rocky was five years and six grades ahead of me, so I tracked
him through the school system quietly, stealthily, avoiding
his pitfalls and false starts, emulating him but at a distance. It
was a role I liked. The younger, the disciple, the pupil, the
neophyte, the ephebe, the apprentice: that's a position people
describe as one of confinement. To me, they have it exactly
wrong. They don't see that it carries a kind of freedom: no
anxiety about finding the path, just the determination to keep
your feet on the path. Most of the time, I've found that challenge enough.

In 1960, when I was in fifth grade, we started to hear about
Africa as part of current events, for the independence movement was sweeping that continent. At home, stories about
Africa and Africans started turning up on TV. We used to
make jokes about Ubangi lips, and poke ours out as far as we
could. The older boys would talk about them, too, in marvel-
ling tones: Black Africans, man, those Africans are *black*, blue-
black. Blacker than Nate or Lawson. Yeah, and those French
women like those Africans too, boy. I saw them arm in arm,
walking down the streets in Paris like it was the most natural
thing in the world—kinky, beady-headed too. Um, um, um.
And they don't want you over there, either. They don't want
you. Dem Africans. They say they're not Negroes; they are
Africans, and don't you call me black. Big-dick motherfuckers
too, swing in trees and shit, living in grass huts.

For my part, I used to watch *Ramar of the Jungle* every
Saturday morning. Ramar was a doctor who looked a lot like

Omar Sharif. His black sidekick, Willy, who looked like Delton Allen, had a pet monkey that perched on his shoulder. Ramar was always being trapped by some witch doctor or medicine man, who was worried because his dances and chants were not reversing the fever of the chief's son. Just one little shot of this, Ramar would tell the chief, and things will be OK. White man's poison, the medicine man would say. Willy, Tom that he was, would betray his people and free Ramar, and the chief's son would live. Ramar would send the son to England to attend medical school. It was *hot* in that jungle too, and the natives would be sweating like crazy, but Ramar in his perma-pressed khaki suit and safari hat would always be clean. Ramar was *bad.* So was Willy's pet monkey.

In school, I was busy learning how to say the names of the leaders of the new African nations: Moise Tshombe, Patrice Lumumba, Kwame Nkrumah, Sékou Touré, Jomo Kenyatta. I'd listen to how Edward R. Murrow or Walter Cronkite said them, then I'd practice in my head. We'd get large current affairs maps each week, with a flat colored map of the world at the top, then a dozen or so news stories numbered to match places on the map. There was a quiz each Friday. I think it was this class that influenced me most to go to Africa when I was nineteen, to live in the bush in a socialist village in Tanzania for a year, and then (with a kid I met from Harvard) to hitchhike across the equator, from the Indian Ocean to the Atlantic Ocean, without leaving the ground.

I lived for that map each week. I loved globes and maps and geography. History too. The only problem with history class was that they'd bring up slavery—for a minute or two at the end of the Civil War section, which was a minute or two of mutual embarrassment. The Africans had been primitive savages, swinging in trees and eating bananas, worshiping rocks and stones and trees, until the White Man came to set them free by granting them admission to the University of

Slavery. John Brown was a crazy troublemaker; the first man to get killed at Harpers Ferry was colored. That showed how very evil it was. Mr. Lincoln got assassinated because he freed the slaves.

Now, that always made me feel bad. Every time one of them tries to help you people too much, Daddy would say, laughing, he gets shot. First was Kennedy—King would be next, he reckoned. The oddest thing about the assassination of President Kennedy, to me—once you got over your shock and tears about him being dead—was the first question that the colored people asked when they heard the news. "Was he colored?" they asked, referring to the President's assassin. My grandparents, my parents, and I would ask that same question, in that same way, upon hearing the news of any tragedy of major dimensions that could implicate the entire race. "Was he colored?" we'd ask, hoping against hope, expecting the worst. "Was he colored?"

9 / Love Junkie

I was a popular enough kid in class. Twenty-four of us started first grade together. By senior year our number had grown to thirty-six, but the original twenty-four were still there, twelve years later and a lot of water over the dam.

Though I had served as class president about four times, I wasn't popular with the girls, not as a potential boyfriend, anyway. Yet Mama's friends, the colored ladies, seemed to like my company, and I loved theirs. I couldn't believe the many ways in which women could be beautiful. The way they smelled, their well-styled hair, the shape of their hips; the edge of a bra under the arm or its X outline revealed under a blouse; a flash of thigh from a crossed leg or a leg uncrossing as it raised itself from a car seat—these were pleasures that struck me with a passion as real as any I've felt at more direct encounters. Especially I loved the reassurance of soft breasts against my chest. Your day will come, Mama's friends would say to me mysteriously. When? I wondered miserably. When I'm sixty?

Actually, I had had several "sexual" experiences when I was five and six and seven, with my cousins and a few neighbors.

The "ands" in those sentences are meant to be cumulative. My cousin Greg and I "got engaged" to Sylvia and Gloria, respectively, up behind Big Mom's house. It is amazing to me that we didn't get caught, taking our pants down and rubbing against each other. We used to play house, doctor, hot dog in the bun, and all the other things we could think up that involved taking off our clothes.

Big Mom, I was convinced, would have had a complete and total heart attack had she happened to learn what was happening just out her back window. The boys bought the girls silver "skeleton" rings, with red "ruby" eyes, from the penny machine. You could do *it*, if you were engaged. Everybody knew that, even us. One time we did get caught, or rather, *I* got caught, with one of the girls by Mama's brother Howard. "What have you been doing, boy?" he shouted, sneaking up the front stairs of Big Mom's house, catching us rubbing together on the floor. "I ought to tear you up," he thundered. "Go home and tell your mother what you been doing."

Was he *crazy*, I wondered. There was no way on earth that I was going to tell *anybody* what me and that girl had just been doing. I went home and asked Mom if I could take a bath. She was delighted. Nice to take a warm bath in the middle of the day, she had said, heating up the teakettle to fill the tin tub. I kept wondering if that black-assed Howard was going to walk in, checking up on me and the state of my confession. As I sat there in those warm suds, considering my fate and its alternatives, common sense suggested strongly that this little experience would remain between me and Howard, if Howard and I had any common sense. But what if Howard said something to Mama? I *dreaded* the thought of seeing him again, and tried to avert my eyes when I did. Of course, Howard was too busy tending to his own business to worry about me.

A male friend my age and I used to rub up against each other, occasionally, when my cousins weren't around. We didn't go in for kissing, but rubbing felt pretty good. One day, when we were taking a shower together at our house on Rat Tail Road, as we often did (he didn't have a shower at his house), he said we couldn't do it anymore. No explanation, just no more rubbing.

And later, it seemed, girls could be so mysterious.

When the girls in my class started having their periods, I didn't have the faintest idea what they were talking about. I didn't know about ovulation, I didn't know about bleeding. I didn't even know where the blood would emerge.

I didn't know for the longest time where babies came out. Mark Cheshire swore that babies came out of a mother's behind, but I knew *that* wasn't right. The stomach, I said. It opens up some kind of way. You're crazy, he said. That was first grade. By seventh grade, my cousin Norma had told me where blood passes out of the body, and how to drive somebody crazy by blowing in her ear and twirling your tongue in it. Norma would have made a fortune as a sex counselor. I learned more about the human body from her in two weeks than I did from all the biology and sex courses I ever attended. The whole thing seemed mystically beautiful to me, especially when the girls in eighth grade spoke about their periods. All the girls used the same scented sanitary napkins in eighth grade, so we knew whose time had come and when it was over.

By our midteens, Greg and I used to chase girls together, especially in Keyser, and especially the honey-colored Hollingsworth girls. Greg was very good-looking, with a nice grade of hair. His father, Uncle Joe, had straight hair like Daddy's, but Greg got more of the straight follicles than I did.

He also got more girls, and more nooky, which wasn't too hard because I didn't get any. Don't get me wrong: I had my passions and flings of the imagination early on, especially with Marjorie Twyman, whose skin bore a dark milk-chocolate sheen and who looked so pretty when she was eating that I would go by her house every day around dinnertime, just to watch her chew. More often than not, I was on the long end of desire and the short end of consummation. My eleventh summer brought Gail Terry from Yonkers, and we took a lot of pleasure in sharing our tongues. But after a few years, the two or three available colored girls in school were more like cousins than potential girlfriends. Besides, I was mesmerized by the unattainable Hollingsworths, on the one hand, and by Linda Hoffman, on the other.

Something never named ended my friendship with Linda when we were about eleven. The strictures of race had entered our lives, catching us unawares. As the age of dating dawned, the fact that it was an impossibility for us did not have to be spoken.

Part of it was that three of us were separated from the rest of the class, and she felt left behind. This happened in the seventh grade. Mr. Beach, "the colonel," who smelled so bad but who loved math like life itself, decided that Pat Amoroso, Katharine Schultz, and I should be skipped to the eighth-grade level of math, which was Algebra I. To accommodate the schedule, we were also placed with the eighth graders in social studies, or "civics." For some reason, he left Linda behind. Linda is smart too, I said to Mr. Beach, longing to take Hoffman along. Thank you for your opinion, he said.

I reached my arm out for her, I called her name aloud, I urged her to catch my hand, but it was no use. I did not have the power to reverse his decision. She was tracked toward home ec (the boys took an extra year of typing). She later told someone that that year did her in. By eighth grade I was taking Algebra II, a year later, it was plane and solid geometry, with the seniors, juniors, and sophomores. Trying to get somebody, anybody, to find me cute. Praying to God to help me get 100s on my tests.

In my mind, Linda and I were still an item. Her girlfriends would ask me on the street if I still liked her. And she even asked me once herself, as we sat on the bleachers over at the high school during practice for the Junior Fair. I was so embarrassed that I shook my head no. And that was that. It's safe to say that I spent the next eight years, and a few more since, trying to erase the memory of the lies pride had led me to speak.

In other classes, Linda and I kept pace at school, but we never could connect again. My mother wanted me to find a nice colored girl, like Jeannie Hollingsworth. And Lord knows I tried. I even joined the bowling league in Keyser, hitchhiking the five miles every Saturday, just to be near Jeannie. After all, she did like athletes, and bowling was just about the only sport in which I could possibly excel.

Linda's parents, like my own, thought better of our friendship, though they always treated me very well, especially her father. Dr. Hoffman died suddenly of a heart attack in the middle of the night when Linda and I were fourteen. "I heard a kind of *thump*," she told me later, at one of the few times we could talk anymore without fighting. "And I knew that he was dead."

I remember that conversation, because our conversations had grown so infrequent by then, and tortured. Linda was my natural girlfriend, I desperately wanted to believe, yet she was distancing herself from me more every day. We learned that we could talk on the phone, even at the worst times, even much later, when we had become warring forces, inflicting pain upon each other whenever and wherever we were able. I could feel her hatred when she saw me, I could feel the fact that she despised me, I could feel her scorn. But not on the phone. I wouldn't call her very much; but when the time was right, when an excuse offered itself, I would be on it, as we'd say, and it would work. Even the flimsiest excuse, like, What pages did Mrs. Iverson give us to read? or, When did she say that book report was due? An exchange that should have taken four or five seconds would last for twenty warm, intimate minutes. I'd rush to school next day to see if the feeling was still there, if at least we'd turned that stupid corner. I'd search her face furtively and hunt in her voice for whatever had been so magical the night before, whatever had made me understand she loved me, knew that my heart was true and that I admired her. But it would not be there.

I can see her face even now, her brown hair and the piercing blue eyes. How could anyone tire of looking into those eyes? All that had been built up in that deliberately improvised telephone conversation had, during the night, unraveled like Penelope's knitting. Her smile was glacial, her eyes were cold and stony. The truce was over. Whatever relationship we had could never be part of our public interaction. In public, she would cut me dead.

I started to read that year, to bridge the gap with Linda. She was the one who ate books. She'd sit in study hall in total concentration, twirling her hair and devouring a book. So I started to read books, too. Oh, I had read books before, mind you, and had read lots of them. But sports books, mostly. I read sports books to get closer to Daddy and Rocky, or at least to know a little of what they were talking about. I did all my book reports on such scholarly titles as *Basketball Bones* and *Last Second Shot*, the sort of thing you could read in an hour.

Of course, it wasn't just Linda's example that made me change. It was my teacher Mrs. Iverson who finally drew the line. Those books you are reporting on are fluff, she declared. You are forbidden to report on them anymore.

Fluff? What was that? And what was I supposed to read instead?

She gave me *A Tale of Two Cities*. I could never read a book that thick, I told her.

Just read it, she said.

I stayed up most of the night reading that book, and I was sorry when I became so sleepy I couldn't read anymore. I went on to *Les Misérables*, to biographies of Einstein, then Schweitzer. I remember the green cover of *Genius in the Jungle*, by Joseph Gollomb. Schweitzer was a revelation: I wanted to learn to play organs and restore them, just as he did. I wanted to walk past a church on the Day of Pentecost on my thirtieth birthday, just as he did, and decide to change my life, secure with the knowledge that I would help the world—and win the Nobel Prize. Treating malaria in Africa would be a natural for me.

I read *My Sweet Charlie*, a tearjerker about a black boy and a white girl who fall in love. He gets lynched, I think, or anyway something tragic happens to him because of white racism, and it all comes to a melodramatic ending. I gave it to Linda. I don't think she appreciated the plot.

And then I read *The Agony and the Ecstasy*, completely enraptured by Irving Stone's divine kitsch. It was I who was carving the Carrara marble with my chisel as if it were mere clay. Best of all, though, was the passage about Michelangelo's making love with his mistress early in the afternoon: especially the part about how he had gone to her house unannounced, how she had answered the door clad only in a robe, which she opened for him when he kissed her, and how red her nipples appeared against her tanned body. I read that page so often, it started to turn yellow from exposure to the light. It was the first time I had been aroused by words on a page, a strange and magical experience. Only reluctantly did I return the book to the library.

On Saturdays, I used to go to the library in Keyser, check out recordings of Shakespeare, and listen to them while I read the plays. I loved the sound of Richard Burton's voice, and the clomping of the horses' hooves in *Macbeth*. Linda Hoffman was impressed by none of this, not even when I told her about Bertrand Russell and the bicycle. It seems that Russell was out riding his bicycle one day, when he decided on the thirty-second turn (more or less) that he didn't love his wife, reasoned that it was only fair and honest to tell her, and headed back to do so. Incredible! I read that passage almost as much as I read the one about Michelangelo's mistress in *The Agony and the Ecstasy*.

The listing of Dell Authors at the back of their books became my own reading list. I remember the color of the pages and the size of the print, their red or black covers. I'd order other books, by people I had heard of even vaguely, and read those too. Picking up a new book at Red Bowls's newsstand was almost as exciting as smelling a new textbook or the mimeographed handouts we used to get in grade school.

I had been going Up the Hill to listen to music with my uncle Earkie the Turkey. He knew women and he knew music, especially R & B and jazz. Sometimes I'd go up "to see Big Mom," and I'd drink her homemade lemonade (squeezed fresh every day), then sit in the darkened front room with Earkie while he played his favorite records on the Victrola. He had mean songs, love songs, and jazz. All colored, of course. For however fried our greased-down, stocking-capped minds might have been in the fifties, *nobody* was confused about the music. Soul. R & B. Silver-tongued crooners, like Nat King Cole. Brook Benton. Ben E. King. Earkie might

I realized then that what I loved about Nat King Cole and Johnny Mathis was their sentimentality, not their processes. The way they made my heart sing. The way they made me sad. I was always singing sad songs, because I was always feeling lonely, always imagining myself in love with someone who did not know I was alive. And then I decided that I was always in that situation because I happened to *like* the feeling of isolation and pain I got when my heart swelled up to burst; and I let it, recollecting myself in the privacy of my room.

Meantime, the list of my infatuations was miles long. Hello. I love you. Will you marry me? My name is Skip. Not a strategy guaranteed to seduce. Why did she run away? I'd wonder, crushed.

I used to go up Keyser to see Terri Sawyer. (When I was little, *nobody* used an *i*; then some model or actress showed up, and things were changed. Terri was probably born Terry Sawyer.) She was funny and had pleasantly rounded hips, the softest, fullest lower lip, and a straight long nose. Stay away from there, Daddy had scolded for reasons I could not understand, coming out of the blue as it did. I refused. After days of wrangling about this, he finally said flatly: "They've got crabs." I looked at him in stunned silence at the idiocy of his remark. What's wrong with that? I asked. We eat crabs all the time. The subject never arose again.

I wasn't sophisticated when it came to sexual jargon. Daddy and I had a run-in over another term: jack off. For some reason I thought it was a cool thing to say, and so I went around saying it, over and over again, as loudly as I could. But what does it mean? I demanded of my father when he insisted that I stop. After what seemed like an eternity, he finally replied that it meant "playing with yourself." He was so embarrassed that he turned heels and left the room. The only thing I could think of, as I watched him disappear so hurriedly, was all the times I'd sat alone on the living room floor, watching Mama hard at work on her Singer sewing machine, while I cut out Betsy McCall dolls and watched *Ding Dong School* or *Romper Room*. Playing with yourself wasn't anything to be ashamed of, I thought, though having a few friends around was infinitely better.

Terri loved me . . . like a brother. She must have said it a hundred times. I had more "sisters" than I knew what to do with: Jeannie Hollingsworth, Sherry Lewis, Sandy Johnson. And the last thing in the world I needed was another sibling. Rocky was hero enough for me. Soon enough, though, my idea of brothers and sisters would take a drastic turn.

10 / Joining the Church

People got all dressed up to go to church, and everybody went: Baptist, Holiness, or Methodist (the Methodist being of an evangelical variety and in most ways indistinguishable from the Baptist). The Gateses, as I have said, were Episcopalians, born into it, Pop would say. And Grandma founded St. Phillips Episcopal Church in 1890. But there was no colored Episcopal church in the Tri-Towns, and Daddy didn't feel welcome at St. James's. The priest had asked him to sit in the back pew, "just until you learn which pews belong to the regular parishioners, you understand." That was all it took. He wouldn't start going there until I joined, in 1966.

Until then, it was Walden Methodist.

I went to church every Sunday, all clean and pressed, greased down and shining, clean as I could be. Even so, I didn't come to like church until I was ten or eleven, unless somebody good was preaching or the choir was singing gospel music—which, to my taste, they did not do enough. "The Prodigal Son," say, or "The Last Mile of the Way." Then church could make you feel good, with people "patting their foots" and nodding their heads and being in tune with the message.

115

But that didn't generally happen at Walden Methodist, which was more staid and sedate than the other two colored churches, especially when Reverend Mon-roe was there. Reverend Mon-roe was a nice guy, medium-brown-skinned, with a not-bad grade of hair, which he combed over to one side, a part being cut in the other side. His wife was blue-black, actually kind of purple, and played the piano. I'd heard about blue-black Negroes but had never actually seen one up close till the Mon-roes came to our church. (There would be a few at the carnival that came to town every summer and had a colored act, including an all-colored strip show.)

What the church did provide was a sense of community, moments of intimacy, of belonging to a culture. I think that's why people went to camp meetings, which were held up in the country, around Williamsport and Moorefield, thirty or so miles from Piedmont. Walden Methodist was too conservative to be involved in such revival meetings, but the Holiness Church was big on them, and you didn't have to be a member of Holiness to go. Anybody could just walk right in and be saved. The big extended tent, the grass freshly cut (by scythes in the old days, by machines today): that was a camp meeting. It was part of the ritual: working hard on Saturday, partying Saturday night, picnic and camp meeting on Sunday—an ideal weekend. Those who understand, on some level or another, the real nature of the ritual don't distinguish between the sacred and the secular. Miss Toot and Mr. Marshall, Eudie and Charlie Stewart, would drink and party and dance all night long at the Legion on Saturday, come home at dawn, bathe and change, then show up a half hour later at Walden Methodist, where Miss Toot would bang out "The Prodigal Son" on that rickety piano like there was no tomorrow. I, for one, thought it sounded better when she was still a little drunk, when the liquor hadn't quite worn off. The distance between the sacred and the secular was the distance between the bathtub and the Legion.

Reverend Mon-roe's predecessor, Reverend Tisdale, was tall and fat, greasy and black, and his highly powdered, light-complected wife played the piano too. Reverend Tisdale used to say Amen loud when somebody put a large bill in the collection plate. (Large was relative in Piedmont; five dollars used to do the trick.) Ain't that awful, people would say to each other, dragging out the words.

I didn't know Reverend Tisdale, because I was too little. But I did know Reverend Mon-roe. Reverend Mon-roe would come to see me as his heir apparent.

One Easter, it fell on me to deliver a "piece" before the congregation, a piece being what we called a religious recitation. I don't know what the folk etymology might be, but I think it reflects the belief that each of the fragments of our praise songs is part of a larger whole. And each of us kids, during a religious program, was called upon to say our piece. Mine was "Jesus was a boy like me, and like Him I want to be." That was it. (I *was* only four.) So after weeks of practice in elocution, hair pressed and greased down, shirt starched and pants pressed, I was ready. Ready to give my piece.

I remember skipping along to the church with the other kids, driving everyone crazy, saying over and over, "Jesus was a boy like me, and like Him I want to be." "Will you shut up!" my friends demanded. Just jealous, I thought. They probably don't even know their pieces.

Finally, we made it to the church, and it was packed—bulging and glistening with black people eager to hear pieces, despite the fact that they had heard all the pieces already, year after year.

Because I was the youngest child on the program, I was the first to go. Miss Sarah Russell (whom we called Sister Holy Ghost—behind her back, of course) started the program with a prayer, then asked if little Skippy Gates would step forward. I did so.

And then disaster struck: I completely forgot the words of

my piece. Standing there, pressed and starched, just as clean as I could be, in front of just about everybody in our part of town, I could not for the life of me remember one word of that piece.

After standing there I don't know how long, spellbound by all those staring eyes, I heard a voice from near the back of the church proclaim, in a marvelous bell-like voice: "Jesus was a boy like me, and like Him I want to be."

And Mama smoothed her dress and sat down. I bowed and slunk back to my seat, as the applause and the laughter resounded throughout our little church.

We called Miss Sarah "Sister Holy Ghost" for a good reason. She talked to the Lord directly—on the phone, in her living room, or wherever she felt like it. The Lord consulted with her on a daily basis, giving her full reports on all the seraphim and the cherubim. So we were convinced. She had a thick neck, very smooth, encircled by three dark folds that ran down to the top of her ample chest. Sweat would collect in those folds when she'd pray. It didn't matter how cold it got; she'd sweat when she prayed.

Prayer was work for Miss Sarah. Uncle Nemo used to say that you could see the prayers bouncing off unbelievers, especially my mama. Miss Sarah would say that you had to believe, or else the prayers couldn't get to Heaven; they'd be trapped up there on the ceiling, swinging around with the Casablanca fans. So she pushed them through, with her chest. She had a way of heaving her bosom and jerking when she prayed, as if the Holy Ghost would erupt when she got on Its wavelength, letting her know that she was on the right path, that she was getting through. They had a close relationship, the Holy Ghost and Miss Sarah.

Miss Sarah would talk about the Father, and talk about the

Son, and do so with the deepest reverence and respect. But the Holy Ghost was her true love. Her ace-boon-coon. Tongues of fire, she'd say, talking about the Day of Pentecost, the day the Holy Ghost came to town and taught people how to talk in tongues and to feel the spirit and to do the Holy Dance like Miss Maggie Walker, who could do the Mashed Potatoes years before Dee Dee Sharp even dreamed of doing it.

Everybody in the Holiness Church—the Church of God in Christ—used to do the Holy Dance. That church would rock, especially when Mr. Les would be playing his saxophone. Before he joined the church, he was the Chuck Berry of the Valley: Chuck Berry could play the guitar and dance at the same time. Not only could Mr. Les play the sax standing on his head, he could play two saxes at the same time and still make the place rock. He played all the dances, even for the white people, until he almost got the table kicked out from under him.

Which wouldn't have been so bad, I suppose, except for the rope that was snugly fastened to his neck on one end and to a big heavy central rafter on the other.

Mr. Les was "up Oakland," a town full of crackers and rednecks, if ever there was one, located on Deep Creek Lake, twenty-five or so miles from Piedmont. They hated niggers up Oakland, like they did "over Fort Ashby"—not the way Pat Amoroso's daddy did, but really and truly. NIGGERS READ AND RUN, Daddy claimed a sign there said. AND IF YOU CAN'T READ, RUN ANYWAY.

Anyway, Mr. Les was up at The Barn, a redneck hangout, flirting with all the white women, gyrating and spinning those sinuous tones, making that saxophone into a snake, a long, shiny, golden snake. A keg of beer apiece for these rednecks and a couple of hours of Les's snake working on their minds and their girlfriends' imaginations was all it had taken. Let's

lynch that nigger, someone finally shouted. And so they did—
or tried to, at least. Somebody called the state cops, and they
busted down the door just about the time they were going to
kick the table out from under Mr. Les and leave him dangling
from the big central rafter. They would have given his horn
back afterward, they said. To his family, they said.

But that's not what made Mr. Les stop playing, go straight,
and join the church. It was the Devil that did that. Les was
playing at the Swordfish, just outside Keyser, going out toward New Creek, 'bout three mile. It was late at night, and
the joint was smoking, and Les was blasting away on his horn.
Now, according to everyone who was there, and everyone
who was not, round about midnight the floor opened up and
the Devil clambered out, coming for to carry Les home, so
he could serenade Old Man Dives and John Wilkes Booth and
everyone who was down there below. So what had the Devil
looked like? Red, with horns and a tail and pitchfork, of course.
That was the Devil. When you see the Devil, son, you know
who you looking at.

Les ran from New Creek over Route 50, down Route 250
to Route 46, where he made that sharp left turn you need to
make to get on the road to Piedmont, traveling at about 250
miles per hour, near as anyone could figure. Les was smoking.
And so was the Devil. According to Daddy—who wasn't
there, of course, because everybody there was white—Les
really didn't know if the Devil was behind him or not, because
he never looked back. When he passed the WELCOME TO
PIEDMONT—POPULATION 2,500 sign, he headed downtown
past the elementary school, then took the tracks for the short-
cut to Paxton Street. He ran up to his bedroom, threw himself
on his knees, then—hour after hour after hour—asked his
Lord to be his personal Savior. We figure he started talking
in tongues at about dawn. They found him like that the next
morning, asleep in an attitude of deep prayer, thankful that

his black behind wasn't smokin' in Hell, where he'd toot that sax for the charred multitudes.

Mr. Les was a good preacher too. That's the reason Uncle Jim didn't mess with him. What's more, Uncle Jim knew that Les had defied the Devil, the day the Devil had come to take him to his home. We used to hear him playing in the Holiness Church as we sat in our pews across the street at Walden Methodist, bored stiff when the choir was singing John Wesley and not the spirituals, or stupefied whenever Reverend Monroe was preaching, which was every Sunday. Reverend Monroe did not know the Holy Ghost intimately and was not on a first-name basis with the Lord. But he was competent: that was the sentiment among those resigned to be his flock.

The truth is, I always avoided the Holiness Church, because I was afraid of the *power* that I knew lived in there. I had seen it in the way that people spoke about the church, the fear and awe in their eyes. I had seen how it had turned people around, even the most unlikely people, like Rocky's classmate Vic Clay. Victor Clay had been a heathen and a hedonist. Then one day, as he tells it, he was walking out of the Holiness Church, was almost out the door . . . when the Spirit came upon him, spun him around, and propelled him back into the sanctuary. It was a camp meeting. Strange things happened at camp meetings.

Having seen the power that could make people forsake the world and stop their sinning—even people who loved dancing like life itself, such as Darnell Allen and my buddy Richard Bruce—I avoided the Holiness Church, because I wanted to put myself out of harm's way. I never wanted to believe *that* much, even at the best of times.

Our Evangelical Methodist church was sedate compared to its sanctified neighbor, but it was certainly not without its own fervor, much of which was provided by Miss Sarah.

Because Miss Sarah was a Holy Ghost person, she loved

reading from Revelations, *loved* the idea of fire and earthquake, apocalypse and destruction. The signs of the times,
she said a thousand times if she said it once, wars and rumors
of wars, famine, earthquakes, but especially "not knowing the
seasons but for the budding of the trees." Man defying the
natural order, first flying and now trying to go to the moon!
Jesus is coming, He's coming *soon*, He's giving us the Signs
of the Times, He'll come like a Thief in the Night. Miss Sarah
was our link with Heaven and the angels, our medium to the
Lord. Get yourselves together, she'd tell everyone, and stop
that dancing and drinking and gambling. Stop that whoring
around. Playing cards. Going to basketball games, and especially dancing up at the Legion.

So I did.

Well, there wasn't any whoring around for me to stop, but
I would have if there had been. Jesus was twelve when he
joined the church, so I would join at twelve. I was ready. I
used to pray a lot. I felt good when I prayed. I used to pray
that I'd get a 100 on a test, straight A's on my report card.
One time I prayed for a fishing pole. I wrote out a prayer on
a piece of paper, folded it up, and forgot it. Then, a few days
later, my uncle (the one with the blue eyes, who went to jail
over that white woman) drove up from Cumberland and gave
me one. Mama found that prayer a few weeks later, read it
out loud at the dinner table, then broke down and cried about
how sweet it was. I wanted to disappear through a hole in the
floor. I couldn't believe she was reading it; I couldn't believe
I got that fishing pole, either. This prayer business was more
powerful and useful than I'd thought.

But now so much more was at stake—not a fishing pole,
anymore, but a matter of personal destiny. Hadn't people
said, for as long as I could remember, that I was special? My
nickname was a truncation of "Skipper," and outlandish as it
sounds, that was the role many people saw for me. Once, I

was downtown at lunchtime, on my way to the Cut-Rate to buy a hot dog with chili, then take it around Back Street to Aunt Marguerite's house, where I'd have lunch with Greg. I walked past Mr. Chili—the man who was famous with Daddy for saying "Don't no man know dat love"—and he pulled me aside to tease me. And then he stopped abruptly, placed his hand on my head and looked into my eyes, and said that I had "not a bad grade of hair," and that if I combed it backward it would look better. As forgettable as the incident must sound, it was the way he looked at me, right in the eyes, and the warmth of his hand on my head, that made me know he thought I was special. It was because I was Pauline Coleman's boy. I have thought often of that moment, and of the comfort it brought, comfort I was soon to need.

IV / Saved

11 / Change of Life

Though I didn't realize it at the time, probably the biggest reason I joined the church was Mama. Mama, who knew so well how life could kill the thing that made you laugh, who remembered at every funeral what a person had hoped to be, not what he had become, seemed to be dying herself, before my eyes.

It came with menopause, and that's how we talked about it. Because we never had the vocabulary to talk about what it turned out to be, a depressive disorder that never quite left her. In fact, she was never the same again, but of course permanence is something you recognize afterward. I can say that a veil passed over her life, dimming her radiance, and then never quite lifted away.

I was twelve and she was forty-six when it started, and it was beyond my comprehension. I only knew that something had eclipsed the woman who gave birth to me and raised me, and that nothing I could do seemed to restore things. I was powerless, and so was she. Mama's "change" was the great crisis in my life, the crossroads of my childhood. I was devastated.

It was when Mama got sick that I began to withdraw from other kids. She'd talk about dying for hours. She told me to prepare for her death. She'd tell me she was in a lot of pain. And then she would cry. No amount of love could help. I'm very sick, she would say, and I believe I'm going to die. You'll live with your father, and things will be OK. But it is important that you prepare yourself, she repeated.

I noticed smaller changes. Mama, the fearless one, suddenly became afraid of dogs. She started to alter physically, as well. Mama used to do exercises devoutly and weighed a trim ninety-eight pounds. At about this time, though, she gained fifty or sixty pounds. Then the clutter in our home started, because she would buy canned goods obsessively, as if to stock a bomb shelter we didn't have. She began to buy cloth too, bolts of material for some future occasion. Before long, there were galvanized garbage cans filled with bolts of cloth. A sense of need, born of a childhood of scarcity, now came upon her, spurring a pack rat's notion of providence— a contained panic about running short. Running out. Going without. Needing and not having. Even as the house became cluttered with her acquisitions, she became obsessed with cleanliness, spending a good part of each day vacuuming. Vacuuming and dusting. I liked trying to help her, and would cook, and clean, and even iron sometimes. I would read the pamphlets that started appearing all over our house, with titles such as "The Phases of Eve" and "The Change of Life," so that I might get a handle on this crazy, evil thing that had entered our lives.

I could not break the spell, no matter how ardently I labored. The depression only deepened that year, and I watched her grow sadder every day.

The night they took her away to the hospital, she hugged me as if that was the end. I cried until I fell asleep, afraid that she would die, afraid that I was responsible. And if I was, as I suspected, responsible, I had a good idea how.

You see, I had developed all sorts of rituals. I would, for instance, always walk around the kitchen table only from right to left, never the other way around. I would approach a chair from its left side, not the right. Mama had hung a beautiful oak crucifix in the hall that connected our bedrooms and the toilet, and I would nod my head as I passed it, just as I had seen my father do at the Episcopal funeral of his father. I got into and out of the same side of bed, slept on the same side, and I held the telephone with the same hand to the same ear. But most of all, as if my life depended on it, I crossed my legs right calf over left, and never, ever, the other way around.

Until one Sunday. For a reason that seemed compelling at the time, probably out of anger or spite, I decided that day to cross my legs in reverse. It was a dare, an act of defiance, a deliberate tempting of fate. And it took place just after Sunday supper, at about 1:00 p.m. Mama had not felt like getting dressed that day. She was having "hot flashes," as she'd started to call them, and felt "disconnected," disembodied from herself. She was going to die, she said to me, over and over and over that day. She'd had one "spell" in the middle of a funeral, just a couple of Sundays before. I wasn't there, but I heard that my aunts Helen and Hazel had taken her out of the church to Hazel's house, where the post-funeral meal was being served. Talking crazy talk, was the way Daddy still describes it. Out of her head.

And on this afternoon, the sense of illness lay so heavy you could have gathered it in your hands like snow and rounded it into balls to throw. We all waited for something terrible to happen. And then it was Mama who told me, through her tears, that she had to go to the hospital, that she didn't know when she would be coming back, and that if she shouldn't come back, I must never forget that she loved me.

She didn't die. After her hospitalization of four or five days she started taking a lot of pills prescribed by the doctors, which accumulated like everything else. She had weathered acute depression, but despite real improvement, she did not emerge healthy and whole, as I had dared to hope. Her phobias would evolve in unpredictable ways. In later years, she developed a fear that objects resting on a table or a countertop would fall off the edge. She would go around the house pushing objects farther back from perilous edges. It puzzled and vexed me: I'd point out, in a reasoning tone, that it would take an earthquake to produce the results she feared. But Mama felt her life had been shaken by just such an earthquake; she knew how easy it was to fall off the edge.

As did I in my own way. My metaphor was an untethered craft, battered by frigid waters, too far out for me to bring back to shore.

But Mama wasn't the only one to change. I could never shake the idea that if only I hadn't dared fate to punish me, by crossing my legs the wrong way around, Mama wouldn't have become sick and gone to the hospital. It was a sense of guilt so enormous that I couldn't talk about it. Except to Jesus. That Sunday when Mama went away, I started to atone. I prayed all day, all evening, and the next day: if God would just let Mama not die, as she was convinced she was going to do, I would give my life to Christ and join the church.

After enough time had passed to show that the Lord had kept His side of the covenant, it fell to me to fulfill mine. When I announced my intention to join the church, Daddy thought I'd taken leave of my senses. Mama, quietly wrestling with her own devils, was more tolerant, of course, but even I saw that she hoped I would outgrow it. If you go into this thing, Daddy said quietly, scarcely able to believe his ears, don't do it halfway. And don't be a quitter. Nobody likes a quitter.

Nobody my age had joined the church in years, at least not the Methodist church. I had been thinking about doing it for several months, since I had turned twelve. It was 1962. Each

time in the service when Reverend Mon-roe would invite all
who wished to make Jesus their personal Savior to come forward and enter the circle, I had been tempted to go. But I
waited until a Sunday afternoon service in Keyser. Reverend
Mon-roe had two churches, you see; he preached at Walden
in Piedmont, but his primary pulpit was in Keyser, and he'd
shuttle from one to the other, preaching in one and then the
other, each Sunday.

I sat there throughout the service, nervous and tense. My
stomach was doing flip-flops. I thought he'd never read the
invitation; I thought he'd never stop that boring sermon.

When finally he did, I found myself rising mechanically,
stumbling out of the pew, wandering to the front of the
church, standing right in front of Ralph Edell Mon-roe, and
wondering what would happen next. Nobody quite knew what
to do. It had been so long since anyone joined the church that
no one could remember what came next. Mon-roe stumbled
through the book of rites until he found the right page, and
then he asked me the prescribed questions.

Do you here, in the presence of God and of this congregation, renew the solemn promise contained in the Baptis-
mal Covenant, ratifying and confirming the same, and
acknowledging yourselves bound faithfully to observe and
keep the covenant, and all things contained therein?

Have you saving faith in the Lord Jesus Christ?

Do you entertain friendly feelings towards all the members of the Church?

Do you believe in the doctrines of the Holy Scriptures
as set forth in the articles of religion of the Methodist
Church?

Will you cheerfully be governed by the Discipline of the
Methodist Church, hold sacred the ordinances of God,
and endeavor, as much as in you lies, to promote the
welfare of your brethren, and the advancement of the
Redeemer's kingdom?

Will you contribute of your earthly substance according
to your ability, to the support of the Gospel, Church,
and poor, and the various benevolent enterprises of the
Church?

Yes, yes, and yes! I answered as forcefully as I could, and
the reverend proclaimed the reception address:

We welcome you to the communion of the Church of
God; and in testimony of your Christian affection and the
cordiality with which we receive you, I hereby extend to
you the right hand of our fellowship; and may God grant
that you may be a faithful and useful member of the
Church militant till you are called to the fellowship of
the Church triumphant, which is without fault before the
presence of God.

Then, departing from the text, he invited everyone in the
church—all of them older women—to march single file to the
front and welcome me into the fold. God bless you, Skippy,
each one said, shaking my hand warmly, or hugging me, or
running her hand over my forehead or across my head. That
part was so beautiful that I couldn't help but cry. I stood there
crying and shaking hands, until everyone had passed by. Then
I sat down again.

The first thing I did after joining the church was to go
down to the Five and Ten Cent Store, to the school-supply
section, where they stocked the boxes of twelve, twenty-four,

and sixty-four Crayola crayons. There I discreetly placed $1.18, in change, down between the neatly stacked cartons. I had stolen a box of crayons when I was six, and wanted to atone for my sin by repaying the store, with interest, for my crime.

I began to cook most of the evening meals for the family. When Mama felt like doing the cooking, I would bake: cakes and corn pudding. I still remember the two Betty Crocker cookbooks she had. They were the same shade of green as the *Webster's Dictionary* that Daddy used for doing the crossword puzzles every day. I loved to cook *with* Mama, just to be near her, to be talking with her. But I was constantly frustrated that we never had all the ingredients a recipe would call for, so I couldn't ever get it exactly right. What is oregano? I'd ask my mother, unsure how to pronounce it. And what in the world was cumin? I'd spend hours searching for a recipe that called only for ingredients that Mama stocked. They were few and far between. Furthermore, Betty didn't season with bacon drippings or ham hocks, and she didn't cook the vegetables long enough to suit us.

For the next two years, I didn't play cards, I didn't go to dances, I didn't listen to rock and roll; I didn't gamble or swear, as my classmates did. I didn't even lust in my heart— except once or twice for Brenda. I went to church, and read the Bible, and spent a lot of time thinking about questions that it turned out Miss Sarah and even Reverend Mon-roe weren't prepared to answer for me.

I enjoyed my time alone: I had to, since I hardly went anywhere during these two years, except for school and church. It gave me distance from Daddy and Rocky, neither

of whom seemed to be crazy about the person I was becoming.
It gave me space to think about Mama's change and a way to
use my prayers to help her. It gave me a way to stop thinking
so much about nuclear war. For the world now seemed a
dangerous place, and the Cuban missile crisis of 1962 provided
bleak confirmation. We all went to bed one night thinking
that we were going to die in some terrible, horrible, nasty
way. I prayed and prayed until I fell asleep. Ain't no use
worrying about bomb shelters, Daddy had said. It won't help
much. I just wanted to be at home when it happened, with
Mama and Daddy and Rocky. I was worried that Daddy might
not get to Heaven, as much as he cussed and played cards.
The church would help with my worries about Vietnam, where
my cousin Jay had been sent. His mother, Aunt Marguerite,
was so upset she stopped reading the papers.

Larger things began to worry me, now. After I became a
Christian and was saved, I was terrified that an angel would
show up in my room, bearing some ominous message from
God, or that such a message would appear in the form of
Writing on the Wall. Miss Sarah would talk of that all the
time. I agonized constantly that a bad-news message from God
would delineate my role in life, my obligations to God and to
our people. That was one of the reasons I was afraid of the
dark. I was terrified of the Visitation that would make me an
agent of salvation. More concretely, I feared that one day I'd
open my mouth and somebody else's voice would come out,
as the Spirit possessed me to do its bidding.

I didn't want it to be like that. I didn't want to be an
automaton controlled by heavenly remote. What I did feel
was that God spoke His will to my heart if I asked what I
should do in a given situation. I still ask, and, generally, I still
hear. Sooner or later.

In those days, I spent long hours wondering about, and worrying about, God, Jesus, being born again, eternal life, Hell, the

Devil, why bad things happen to good people, why good things happen to bad people, and what is right and what wrong.

In the end, as I say, joining the church gave me a space of my own, and I found solace in that solitude, long after I realized that the time had come to part ways with our small white wooden church.

12 / Eternity

A man is talking to the Lord, trying to fathom His infinitude. "Lord," he asks, "what's a million years to you?" "A million years is a second to me," the Lord explains. "And a million dollars?" A penny, the Lord replies. "Lord," the man proceeds to ask, emboldened, "would you give me a million dollars?" "Sure," the Lord replies. "Just a second."

When I was in the church, between the ages of twelve and fourteen, staying at home and praying a lot, I used to try to imagine how long eternity could be. "A thousand years is like the blink of an eye to the Lord," Miss Sarah Russell would say. One day, our eighth-grade science teacher, Mr. McGoye, told us that to begin to imagine the length of eternity, we should think of a hummingbird. This hummingbird lands upon a huge stone once every five hundred years. The stone is five hundred miles high, five hundred miles wide, and five hundred miles thick. And once every five hundred years, this tiny little hummingbird lands on this rock and sharpens its beak. The length of time it takes the hummingbird to file down that huge stone to the size of a pebble is the equivalent of *one second* of eternity. He stopped the entire class dead with that one. Especially me. (Only later, when I encountered a similar passage in Joyce's *A Portrait of the Artist as a Young Man*, did I realize that such imagery enjoyed considerable currency.)

Sitting up in Heaven with Miss Sarah and Reverend Monroe for *that* many years, listening to Mr. Lynn Allen and Mr. Doug Twyman argue about whose turn it was to say the morning prayer, was about as appealing as getting a typhoid shot in your behind every day. Who ever thought eternity was a good idea in the first place?

I suppose the shake-up of my spiritual creed was hastened by my realization that I was religious in part because I was scared, scared of Jesus coming back to earth and sending me to Hell, scared of being liquidated or vaporized in a nuclear holocaust, scared of what was happening to my mother— scared, in all likelihood, of life itself.

Uncle Harry, that is, the Reverend Harry A. Coleman, talked me into going to church camp at the end of the summer of my thirteenth year. He and a buddy he'd studied with at Boston University Seminary in the fifties decided to hold a Methodist retreat for teenagers somewhere "up in the country," which means somewhere in Grant or Hardy county, near Williamsport, where Big Mom was born. What I most remember about that camp was sitting by the big campfire and staring longingly into the dark-brown eyes of Eileen Redman, hoping that by some act of the Good Lord Himself this angel of beauty would fall in love with me while we all sang "Kumbaya."

Also memorable that August was a touch football game during which I noticed a sharp pain in my knee. I decided it would be best to retire from the field.

The pain would not go away. I tried elastic wraps and liniment, Deep Heat and Aspercreme, exercising it and resting it, and still it would not go away. I went to see one Dr. Reeves, and he said I had pulled a muscle. I went to see his brother, the other Dr. Reeves, and he said I had torn a ligament. The first Dr. Reeves gave me a cane to use. The second gave me a set of crutches. I was still on them in September when school started. Mr. McGoye, who made beautiful colored chalk drawings of the inside of flora and fauna on the blackboard, started calling me Gimp and Gold Brick.

I was having lunch one day, just across from the high school, at the only sandwich shop over in the Orchard. It had been segregated, until Mrs. Wattie came to town. She was the typing teacher, whom everyone called Mrs. Watusi behind her back. She was young, and she was pretty, but most of all, she was black. Mr. Staggers, the principal, had told the manager of that shop that if Dolores Wattie couldn't eat there, no teacher would eat there, and the place integrated, just like that.

I sat at a table all by myself, since most of the kids went home for lunch. Eating out was not a big concept in Piedmont. They don't want us in there anyway, colored people would say as they drove down the highway, passing restaurants, pulling over at rest stops to munch on picnic lunches in their cars. (One shivery fear possessed us: we believed that if we went to eat where we weren't wanted, they'd spit in our food before serving it.)

But there I was in the freshly integrated sandwich shop, a living, munching symbol of the new dispensation. Martin Luther King come to Piedmont.

I looked over to watch Mrs. Houchins, the gym teacher, who had a beautiful aquiline nose and a charming gap between her front teeth. She was perky and alert and had a large, warm laugh. She also wore short skirts and tight blouses, so she was the favorite work of art among the ninth-grade boys. I watched her crumble a packet of crackers while it was still wrapped in cellophane, then dump the contents into her bowl of chili. It was such a neat trick that I thought how very clever she was. I watched her eat that bowl of chili, and she let me watch her, rolling her spoon over her lips as if that chili were her last meal and my eyes were her final testament.

I limped happily back toward school. We were having an assembly at one o'clock, and I wanted to get a good seat. I was doing fine until I passed the swimming pool.

Three or four feet from the swimming pool's double doors, I ran into a wall of pain. It seemed to rise up out of the earth, surrounding me on all sides. I was inside that pain, and it was inside me. I couldn't move outside the pain, I couldn't shake it off. It wasn't like when you hit your funny bone hard and think you'll lose your mind for a minute. And it wasn't like bumping your head on an overhang, or twisting your ankle, or stubbing your toe. It wasn't *like* anything. This kind of pain lived in its own dimension, and I could hardly see because of it. To move was only to make it worse, left or right, up or down. I was frozen in midstep.

Petie Ross was the first to come by. Petie was black as slate, twice my size, and mean as the day was long. I was as frightened of him as everybody else was. But even Petie sensed that this was no time to play. He grabbed another boy and told me to use the two of them like crutches, and they would carry me to school. On the count of three they lifted. My scream scared even Petie. He sent for the principal. And for Petie Ross to call for Mr. Staggers was like Al Capone summoning Eliot Ness. I *knew* I must be sick. It seemed to take an hour to get me into the back seat of the taxi that had been called. I screamed again when it crossed the tracks, each bump like a hammer drilling deep inside me. I was very afraid.

"It's a torn ligament in your knee," the surgeon said, ignoring completely the fact that my hip joint was disconnected.

(One of the signs of what I had—a "slipped epithesis"—is intense knee pain, I later learned.) So he scheduled me for a walking cast.

I was wheeled into surgery and placed on the operating table, where the surgeon proceeded to wrap my leg with wet plaster strips that would dry into a hard cast, like white concrete. As he worked, he asked questions about my schoolwork, I guess to make the time pass.

"Boy," he said, "I understand you want to be a doctor."

"Yessir." You always said "sir" to white people—unless you were trying to make a statement.

Had I taken a lot of science courses? he wanted to know.

I said, "Yessir. I enjoy science."

"Are you good at it?"

"Yessir, I believe so."

He said, "Tell me, who was the father of sterilization?"

"Joseph Lister."

Then he asked who discovered penicillin.

Alexander Fleming, I answered.

And what about DNA?

Watson and Crick.

The interview went on like this. I thought my answers might get me a pat on the head. Actually, they just confirmed a medical judgment he'd come to.

That's why he stood me on my feet and insisted that I walk. But with the best intentions in the world, there are some things you can't do when your ball and socket are completely separated. So it's not surprising that the joint sheared and I fell on the floor in agony. I wasn't a doctor, but even I figured out something wasn't right.

The doctor shook his head and walked over to my mother, who was waiting in the corridor. "Pauline," he said, his voice kindly but amused, "there's not a thing wrong with that child. The problem's psychosomatic. Because I know the type, and the thing is, your son's an overachiever."

Now, there's an interesting history to that term, and what it meant in Piedmont in 1964 wasn't what it usually means today. Back then, "overachiever" designated a sort of pathology: the dire consequence of overstraining your natural capacity. A colored kid who thought he could be a doctor—just for instance—was headed for a breakdown.

What made the pain abate was my mother's reaction. You have to understand that I'd never, ever heard my mother talk back to a white person before. And doctors, well, doctors were sacred, and their word was scripture.

Not this time. After the doctor said his piece, Pauline Gates stared at him for a moment and announced her decision. "Get his clothes, pack his bags—we're going to the University Medical Center." That was sixty miles away, in Morgantown.

Which wasn't great news as far as I was concerned. The one thing I knew was that they only moved you to the University Medical Center when you were going to die. I was inconsolable.

But it turned out Mama was right. And I wasn't going to die. I had three operations in the course of that year. After the first, in which the joint was pinned together with a metal pin, I walked on crutches for six weeks and began to lose even more weight than I'd lost in the hospital. By the time I got back to school, I was four or five weeks behind. This was not a major problem, except in geometry. I was scared about geometry anyway; I was taking it with the juniors and seniors, and wasn't sure how smart I really was. Low expectations, stay quiet, observe everything. The problem was that I couldn't figure out how $a^2 + b^2$ could *always* equal c^2, until the day when I realized that the letters referred to the sides of a right triangle and c was the hypotenuse. Once I figured that out, learning geometry became one of the most pleasurable experiences of my educational life. I loved its order and logic; I loved making a formal proof. I loved learning its axioms and lemmas. I loved coming to visualize three-dimensional structures on a flat plane.

By the time we got to the unit about 5-12-13 triangles, the doctors had decided that the steel pins they had inserted in my hip had failed. I would need a second operation to remove the pins, and then a third operation in June.

Following the last procedure, a "cup arthroplasty"—a metal ball on the hip—I was confined to bed for six weeks, immobilized by a complex system of weights and pulleys, unable to attend to even the simplest of bodily movements or functions. It was six weeks of bondage—and bedpans. It was also when I had my first glimpse of eternity.

Eternity is a fourteen-year-old strapped down to a bed, held rigidly in place by traction and a system of pulleys and weights, unable to move to the left or to the right, to lift up his body beyond forty-five degrees, unable to turn over, unable to use the bathroom . . . for six weeks. Forty-two long, hot days. One thousand and eight hours. In my mind, that little hummingbird flew back and forth, sharpening its beak on the promontory.

Each day for six weeks, my mother would walk up the big hill in front of the hospital and sit with me from nine to nine, from the time they allowed her in until the time they sent her home. I spent my time quarreling with her. She had rented a small room—which we could ill afford—in a motel that was reserved for the families of patients, just down the hill from the medical center.

Every day, in the middle of the latest quarrel, I'd insist that she go back to Piedmont—or she would insist that she was going back to Piedmont. I think we both came to realize that this was a sort of ritual. I didn't like being a patient, and stoicism wasn't my strong suit. We'd argue about everything and anything—even about what time of day it was—but the arguments kept me from thinking about that traction system.

And maybe they helped her escape her own darkening obsessions.

I learned to play chess there; the doctors would come and play with me, especially a surgeon from the Philippines, a brown-skinned man with dark, wavy hair. He'd drop by, we'd make two or three moves, he'd disappear on his rounds, then he'd return just as abruptly as he'd left. I enjoyed his company, enjoyed the fact that I could give him a run for his money, at least on the chessboard.

I had to learn to walk again, after relearning how to use all the atrophied muscles in my right leg. One day, the chief surgeon asked me to move my leg, using a system of pulleys that had been installed the previous day. After six weeks of nonmovement, to lift my leg even with the pulley was agonizing. He shook his head and said that it didn't look good for an early release for me, until I could retrain those muscles.

I was horrified. I had to get out of that bed. Using a bedpan, and needing an orderly to clean your body afterward, is not much fun. (The orderlies, for their part, were sensitive to my embarrassment and vulnerability. One of them happened to mention to me one day that toilet paper had been invented in 1859. It has become a crucial date for me: 1859. B.T.P. and A.T.P: Before Toilet Paper and After Toilet Paper. It made me wonder about people's toilet habits before 1859. What was Frederick Douglass up to when he used the bathroom in 1842, just before his big speech? Or Plato? Or Shakespeare? Or Shaka Zulu?)

Finally, that day came when the surgeon challenged me to retrain my leg muscles. Almost as soon as he and the interns and the resident had left my room, I decided to try my leg muscles once more. It hurt like hell. I set my jaw and pulled again, slowly this time, ever so slowly but gently and steadily, until my knee bent at a forty-five-degree angle as it was supposed to do. It hurt so much that I asked Mama to leave. I did it again, even more slowly, then again. And again. I'd rest a bit, massage myself, and do it again. By the time the surgeon made his rounds the next day, I could pull up that leg as easily as I wanted to. Hey, Doc, I said, look at this! What's next?

I liked my medical team, mostly because they answered my questions. They talked with me. Fear is everywhere in a hospital. All those hours of the night and day, waiting for a surgeon to come by, then getting five minutes, maximum, to allay your concerns, and spending the next twenty-three hours and fifty-five minutes scared and anxious.

But in some ways the most important words I received were not medical but religious. While I was in the medical center, a new Episcopal priest in Keyser would drive the two hours or so it took to see me in Morgantown. Father Smith had fat jowls and a red face. I liked his robust laugh and his fat, jelly-shaking sides. The flesh of his neck hung around the edge of his collar like dough for a pie crust that hasn't yet been trimmed. The word he bore was that I could drink, smoke, curse, and still be a good Episcopalian. I could even date girls. Now, *that* part was beginning to appeal to me. In fact, the whole thing appealed to me. I wanted to have a spiritual life without being imprisoned by it. I wanted to be a religious person, but I no longer wanted to be a member of Walden Methodist, with its oppressive literalisms.

By this time, the worst of Mama's depression appeared to be over, though it would return in a few years. Her regimen of hormones and other medications had restored her to a reasonable semblance of normality. The woman who stood up to the doctor in the Keyser hospital and who watched over my recuperation at the medical center was the mother I was afraid I had lost. And her own measure of recovery helped to free me from my commitment to the restrictive fundamental-ism that I had so desperately embraced.

What happened during my hospital stay sealed my decision,

but it is clear to me that my disenchantment had been brewing for a while. Part of it was about my growing alienation from my younger Coleman uncles. The more I succeeded in school, the more I rejected their advice, the more bitterly we argued, the quieter they got around me, at least about my successes— though they got louder about my racial politics and my growing discomfort with the Vietnam war. I had been tiring of Miss Sarah, Reverend Mon-roe, and the Methodist church. It was as if I had outgrown a good pair of trousers, my favorite trousers, and had no others to put on. I wanted to learn how to be a free Negro and to be a man, how to be in the world and with God, how to question values and tradition without being kicked out of the fold, how to value community and order, family and the group, yet not have to suppress my uncertainties, doubts, ambivalences in order to be accepted. Soon church for me was only the music, and only Miss Toot's gospel choir at that.

Father Smith seemed to understand all this. He gave me books to read—all kinds of books. Prayer books and catechisms, philosophical and historical works about the church, books like *The Secular City* and *The Other America. Are You Running With Me, Jesus?* blew me away because this priest was talking to God just like He was one of the boys. Anything even remotely like this would have been heresy to Miss Sarah. She would have gotten down on her knees and prayed to Jesus to help me see the light. God became for me a spirit or force that guides, rather than Rex Ingram in *The Green Pastures*.

Father Smith treated me as an equal in conversation; and he didn't think an awakening skepticism was inconsistent with an adolescent's underlying faith. He seemed to offer an intellectual framework to go with my spirituality. Plus, I didn't see why God should mind if I saw the occasional movie, listened to popular music, or took a turn, however ungainly, on the dance floor. My brother used to claim that I checked into the hospital with a Bible in one hand and a cross in the other, then checked out with a deck of cards and a saxophone.

Eventually, I was released from that bed of Procrustes. For the next six months, I walked on crutches; then I used a cane. Gradually, a cane became part of my identity, as did orthopedic shoes with a lift in the right heel. I regarded them with a feeling of despair. Having been freed from the corrective shoes of my boyhood, I was consigned to them again. Finding shoes that did what they were supposed to do and still looked half decent was a difficult business. Each year, it seemed, I needed more of a lift to balance myself, as the metal ball on my hip migrated farther north. In time, I myself would follow suit.

13 / Living
Under Grace

It was at Peterkin, an Episcopal church camp in West Virginia that I attended that summer—the summer of 1965—and the two summers following, that I was given an opportunity to explore the contours of my new faith, and the world beyond Piedmont.

Spending two weeks at Peterkin, made possible by a scholarship, was like stepping into a dream world. It was populated by well over a hundred seemingly self-confident, generous-spirited teenagers, their ages ranging from fifteen to eighteen; they were rebellious, worldly, questioning, cosmopolitan, articulate, bold, and smart. I learned so much at that camp, I don't even know where to begin.

Following a regular regime of breakfast, morning prayers in the chapel, cleanup, seminars, then lunch, we'd sit for long hours in the afternoon, playing hands of bridge, which I was learning as I went along. We'd play on the front porch of the main house, which used to be an elegant hunting lodge, complete with a huge stone fireplace. I had beginner's luck: a couple of small slams, a grand slam, hands with lots of points. We'd play, the four of us—Tandy Tully and her boyfriend,

Peter Roberts, Andrea Strader and I—all afternoon sometimes, watching the other campers come and go, and we'd
talk about this and that and everything, books and ideas,
people and concepts. The war in Vietnam. Smoking. The
existence of God.

Andrea was smart and well-read, intuitive and analytical.
She was also beautiful, cocoa-colored, with a wide plum-pur-
ple mouth that tasted delicious. It was Andrea who told me
early on that I should go to prep school, and then to the Ivy
League. (What's a prep school? I asked her.) That I should
travel and read this and that. She was petite and elegant, and
she sang like an angel. Every night we'd have a campfire, and
every night I'd sit next to her, trying to learn the words of the
traditional gospel songs and the camp songs, listening to my
past and future through Andrea's lovely voice. She had large
black eyes and long, straightened hair that was soft to the
touch. I couldn't believe that she even existed or that she
would want to be with me.

The third black camper at Peterkin was Eddie James—
Edward Lawrence James, The Third, thank you very much.
Eddie was rich. His grandfather had founded a produce business in Charleston at the turn of the century, and it had
prospered. Everybody in Charleston knew and respected the
Jameses, he let us know. All the Democratic politicians kissed
Mr. James II's black behind. Money can't erase color, Andrea
would explain to me, but sometimes it can help you blend a
bit better. The Jameses were proof of that. Eddie was dating
a white girl at camp, which was giving the director, Mary Jo
Fitts, fits. She chain-smoked so much that her teeth looked
like yellow fangs, and her personality matched her teeth.

Sex was everywhere at Peterkin—everywhere but in my
bed. Maybe it could have been there, but I didn't know it,
and I didn't know how to put it there. I was fond of making
all sorts of lofty pronouncements, like: I'm naturally high, or

I'll wait to do it until I get married. I was the walking, talking equivalent of those wall plaques that you can buy in Woolworth's that attest to such sentiments as "M Is for the Many Things She Gave Me" or "Lord, Help Us to Accept the Things We Cannot Change." I wonder how people could stand me. But I was being honest, in the same way that people who collect paintings on black velvet are being honest. I thought I was thinking the right things, remaining pure of heart. I was terribly earnest: the Pentheus of Peterkin. Meantime, everybody else was getting down with somebody or other. You could feel the sexual energy flowing. There was a charge in the air.

A month shy of my fifteenth birthday, I felt I had died and gone to Heaven. I was living in a kingdom, one of the princes. We drank ideas and ate controversy. Is God dead? we asked. Can you love two people at the same time? I feasted on the idea of learning about the world and being a citizen of it.

And yet my sense of this citizenship would be jeopardized not long after I arrived. After a solid week of complete isolation, a deliveryman bringing milk and bread to the camp told the head counselor that "all hell has broken loose in Los Angeles" and the "colored people have gone crazy." He handed him a Sunday paper, which screamed the news about Negroes rioting in some place called Watts. Andrea had overheard and was the one to tell me. Your soul brothers have gone totally crazy, she said. Rioting and shit. I stared at the headline: NEGROES RIOT IN WATTS. We were all trying to understand what was really happening, forced to judge from one screaming headline.

I was bewildered. I didn't understand what a riot was. Were colored people being killed by white people, or were they killing white people? Watching myself being watched by all the white campers, I experienced that strange combination of power and powerlessness that you feel when the actions of another black person affect your own life, simply because you both are black. I realized that the actions of people I did not know had become my responsibility as surely as if the black folk in Watts had been my relatives in Piedmont, just twenty or so miles away.

Sensing my mixture of pride and discomfiture, a priest handed me a book later that day. From the cover, the wide-spaced eyes of a black man transfixed me. *Notes of a Native Son*, the book was called, by James Baldwin. Was this man the *author*, I wondered, this man with a closely cropped "natural," with brown skin, splayed nostrils, and wide lips, so very Negro, so seemingly comfortable to be so?

From the book's first few sentences, I was caught up thoroughly in the sensibility of another person—a black person. It was the first time I had heard a voice capturing the terrible exhilaration and anxiety of being a person of African descent in this country. The book performed for me the Adamic function of naming the complex racial dynamic of the American cultural imagination. I could not put it down.

It became all the more urgent to deal with the upheaval I had felt when I read that headline.

We were pioneers, people my age, in cross-race relations, able to get to know each other across cultures and classes in a way that was unthinkable in our parents' generation. Honest hatreds, genuine friendships, rivalries bred from contiguity rather than from the imagination. Love and competition. In school, I had been raised with white kids, from first grade. To speak to white people was just to speak. Period. No artificial tones, no hypercorrectness. And yet I have known so many Negroes who were separated from white people by an abyss of fear. Whenever one of my uncles would speak to a white person, his head would bow, his eyes would widen, and the smile he would force on his lips said: I won't hurt you, boss, an' I'm your faithful friend. Just come here and let ole me help you. Laughing much too loud and too long at their jokes, he assumed the same position with his head and his body as when he was telling a lie.

But there, at Peterkin, on that day especially, we were all trying to understand what had just happened and what it might mean for our lives, and to do so with a measure of honesty.

What the news of the riots did for us was to remind everybody in one fell swoop that there was a racial context outside Peterkin that affected relations between white and black Americans; we had suddenly to remember that our roles were scripted by that larger context. We had for a blissful week been functioning outside these stereotypes of each other— functioning as best we could, that is—when all of a sudden the context had come crashing down upon us once again. I hated that newspaper. But we overcame it: with difficulty, with perseverance, we pushed away the racial context and could interact not as allegories but as people. It felt like something of an achievement.

I didn't want to leave. I cried when I had to go . . . but then everybody cried. When I got home, my wonderful room full of books and records looked like Cinderella's hovel must have, when she returned from the ball at half-past midnight. My beautiful mountain valley on the banks of the mighty Potomac looked like a dirty, smelly mill town, full of people who cared more about basketball and baseball and eating than anything else. Somehow, between the six weeks of the hospital and the two weeks of Peterkin, some evil blight had stricken my magical kingdom. It made me heartsick, especially the once or twice I was foolhardy enough to try to explain all this to Linda Hoffman or to Johnny DiPilato. There are *lots* of nice church camps, was all that Hoffman said.

It was in 1966, between my first summer at Peterkin and my second, that I gave up the evangelical Methodist Church for

good. It happened on the afternoon that Rocky prevailed upon
me to flout my renunciation of cinema in favor of Heaven and
dragged me down to Searstown at Cumberland to see *A Hard
Day's Night*. He had come back from college for the weekend.
I had *heard* of the Beatles, but that was about it. When I came
out into the light after the movie, which I'd watched with
excitement mingled with a certain dread, I took a sidelong
glance at the sky. I was as disappointed as I was relieved when
no lightning came down to smite me. I almost wanted to see
a heavenly show of displeasure.

I joined Father Smith's church in Keyser. I was grateful to
him for visiting me in the hospital; and he was a good priest,
a village priest. Years later, he would come to my graduation
from Yale, even though he had by then left the priesthood.
(When he was replaced by Fred Bannerot, a Yalie from
Charleston who bragged about being rich, lent me five hundred dollars to pay my expenses at Harvard Summer School—
then told half the town about it—I made my final church
membership move and joined St. James's in Westernport,
closer by, so that Mama, Daddy, and I could walk to church
on Sundays and so we could integrate, at last, the last bastion
of high-church white men left in our branch of the Potomac
Valley.)

Mama and I were confirmed at the same ceremony, at
Peterkin. I never saw my father happier at something I did,
or prouder. Aunt Beck had stood for me as my godmother. I
cried on that day just as I had down at the Methodist church
when I joined. Now my father and I started to attend church
together.

Ironically, it was becoming an Episcopalian that killed the
idea of becoming a minister for me. I had gained the freedom
within the church to question just about anything and everything I wanted to, but I found that I did not want to do this
from the pulpit. I thought that I needed someone to assuage

my doubts, rather than being secure enough to assuage the doubts of others. Besides, I am not fond of uniforms.

The Episcopal Church wasn't without its drawbacks. Some of its songs were lifeless and its sermonic style tended toward the pallid. But it compensated for such failings by its theological freedom, its willingness to let its parishioners range intellectually. Bishop James Pike had even written a book asking *Is God Dead?* without being thrown out of the priesthood or burned at the stake. I liked the prayers; I liked the church's calm and order; I liked the piety of its hymns. I liked the social activism of the young priests of the sixties and seventies, especially that of Father Smith. I loved praying on my knees, right there in church, and taking Communion with real wine, passed in one chalice, hand to hand and mouth to mouth. I loved doing holy days with special services and specific prayers. I loved learning about the history of the holy days, which together spelled out the history of the church itself.

Daddy was delighted when I joined his church, but he didn't want to gloat for fear of jinxing things. Miss Sarah Russell, Sister Holy Ghost, called and pleaded with Mama and Daddy, then shook her head sadly and told me she would pray for me. Uncle Jim said that the Episcopal Church wasn't even a true church, and why didn't I come on across the street with him, Reverend Monk, and Mr. Les, and "become Holiness"? As for me, I felt so much more comfortable in the world, so much more that I belonged in it, than I had before. And I found I didn't miss the Walden Methodist Church much, either, except when I thought about Miss Toot's sublime rendition of "The Prodigal Son" and when I went to funerals.

V / Negro Digest

14 / Just Talking
to the Lord

I loved Uncle Jim—let me say that from the start—and he loved me. He wasn't crazy about Daddy, though, and the feeling, I think it's fair to say, was mutual.

Now, Uncle Jim, as I've explained, was ole Griff Bruce's son, and Griff Bruce was a hunter's hunter. Everybody said that. And, as I have noted, there's a lot of intermingling and intermarrying in hollows, because the gene pool there is so small and desire is so huge. All people in the country have to do is eat, sleep, work, work, work, and make love. So Griff and all the Bruces, Howards, and Cliffords are full of white and Indian blood—and not just West Indian blood. All you have to do is *look* at them; do your own genetic research, with your own eyes. Indian hair, high cheekbones, and a funny ruddy-Negro color. Rhiney, it's called. Negroes with green eyes.

I cite Griff's Indian blood only because everybody else cited it to explain his great abilities in the woods. A hunter's hunter, he was. And Jim—known also as Nemo, after the cartoon character Captain Nemo—had the gift too. In addition to being the spitting image of ole Griff, he somehow inherited his knowledge of the woods. Nemo hunted and fished like he *owned* the woods, all the fish and fowl, the flora and fauna. And when I went out with him, I felt like I owned the woods too. I didn't want to have his skills; I only wanted to be able to enjoy him honing his skills.

Most colored people, when I was growing up, used to claim descent from Indians. And embarrassing as it is to admit, I did, as well, blood rushing to my face, purple as a beet, lying my behind off.

Nemo didn't look Indian. Rather, he looked like a handsome bullfrog, because of his large, wide head and his bulging eyes. When he'd be caught in a contradiction or a lie, his chin would automatically drop onto his chest, and he'd stare out at you with his pop-out eyes. "Hunh?" he'd say, invariably. "Nigger's lyin'," Pop would say. Nemo would not have been good on the witness stand.

He was in the navy in World War II and he was an excellent swimmer. He taught all the colored kids to swim in the river. The pool was segregated until 1956, when I started school, but the creeks and branches were wide open to everybody. He was the scoutmaster of colored Troop 54; he was the first Negro Eagle Scout. And of course, he hunted and fished like nobody's business. Not only was he the first colored man in Piedmont to own guns, but he got guns for everyone in the family. He hunted in all the best hunting places and was not shy about approaching white people for permission to hunt on their land. Which is surprising to me only because he was *deathly* afraid of white people. His fear and Mama's hatred— flip sides of the same coin.

By the time we grew close, Nemo had become the Chief and Principal Servant of the Lord, if not on the Entire Earth, then at least in These Environs. His God was one jealous Dude, and Nemo was His mouthpiece, Nemo the very Fire and Spirit that was His Tongue. Nemo did not play when it came to the Lord. And Nemo had been a player.

"You name it, I did it." There was a certain satisfaction in
the way he'd say these words to me, almost always in his small
motorboat with its Sears, Roebuck motor, just big enough for
three. Women used to like me, he'd say, because I was so
big. That's what Hattie Mae used to say.

I should explain that Hattie Mae was Lazarus Brown's wife
and had been running Dan Adams for nobody knew how long.
Dan was said to be the father of a couple of her children,
which everybody colored in the Tri-Towns and Keyser knew,
if only because the boys all looked like Dan. John turned into
the suffering cuckold, "dying" all my life and working triple
overtime at the paper mill just so he wouldn't have to go home
to that four-room house full of Hattie's mother, the five kids,
Hattie's big black behind, and of course Dan's shadow everywhere. They might not have been so crowded if Dan hadn't
moved his spirit in. Eventually, John and Hattie would find
the Lord, by way of Jehovah's Witnesses.

Nobody makes him stay there, I'd overhear Daddy saying
to Mama. He ain't chained to that blue-gummed woman. She
sure must have some sweet *pussy*, he'd trail off, cuz she's two-
timing, funky, and ugly with it. Um, um, um. Even my mama
would bust up at that.

The Colemans were the first among the colored to be allowed hunting licenses and their own rifles and shotguns. And
they used them too. Deer season and turkey season were
family holidays, for the men. Almost everybody took off the
first day of deer season, and that included most of the kids at
school. Killing a deer was tantamount to slaying a dragon. Just
seeing a deer was a wondrous thing for us, when I was growing
up. It was like seeing a white buffalo or some magical beast,
like a unicorn. But Uncle Jim could spot them no matter how
thick the foliage or how subtle the camouflage. He would
bring his rickety green jeep almost to a halt, able to move it
slowly without startling a skittish doe or buck. There, he'd
say. Look over there, to the right of that old spruce tree,

thirty degrees to the right. Greg and I would look and look, for what seemed like hours, till finally Nemo would say "Ka-pow!" as he fired his imaginary shotgun, and the deer would run away. Deer were wild then, and frightened. The people in the valley used them for food, and those deer knew it.

They also knew Uncle Jim. They *had* to know him. We used to imagine their great war councils, plotting strategy against Mr. Big Jim, king of the mighty hunters. He was a triple-threat man: he could kill them with a gun, kill them with a bow, or kill them with his bare hands, if one was ever dumb enough to get that close to him. He could smell the deer, could Nemo, as well as they could smell him. And he could make turkey calls, all the hunters in the valley would joke, that only the turkeys could hear.

The woods would cooperate with him; the elements were on his side. Or maybe he was on the side of the elements. It didn't matter if it was raining or snowing, sunny or cloudy, cold or warm, dark or light: Nemo got his deer—a few more, actually, than the law permitted. So if you went out with him on the first day of deer season, most probably you'd get one too—one of *his*, since to shoot more than one was against the law.

Nemo wasn't all that big on the law when it came to shooting deer, rabbits, or squirrels, and catching fish. "Nephew, there's man's laws," he'd allow, his voice trailing off. "And then there's God's laws." God, of course, put all those animals on earth to be killed and eaten, and a great number of those unfortunate souls deposited in the Potomac Valley were put there to be killed and eaten by Uncle Jim. He would justify killing so many animals in terms of the difference between God's law and man's law: Thou shalt not kill applied only man to man. (Uncle Jim was a wizard at biblical exegesis, explaining the difference between the quick and the dead as a distinction between those who could react swiftly enough when the Good

Lord appeared on the horizon on Judgment Day—the quick—and those who would be caught unawares—the permanent and everlasting dead. I liked that one a lot, especially when he'd flick his hands to demonstrate what quickness was.)

When you hunt for deer, you sit and wait in some sort of "blind," downwind. You wait for the deer to come to you, rather than stumbling through the woods, scaring them away. Unless, that is, you're hunting at night, in which case you look for them, because if you find one you can blind it with a flashlight, whereupon it "freezes." It's called night-lighting, or jacklighting. Once it's frozen, you could walk up to it and bump it on its head.

One night, Jim and Mr. Bump, the white man who was his running buddy, got caught by the game warden night-lighting some deer. Mr. Bump got away, except for his left shoe, which came off as he disappeared into the darkness of the woods (he said the game warden shot it off). Uncle Jim, less fleet, was arrested. His fine was five hundred dollars, which was a lot of money to pay back then, especially for one deer. Farmer Johnson, the head of the union at the paper mill, arranged a loan with the credit union, that tiny, narrow office building in Westernport that supplied so many of the workers' needs. The story became a legend; Mr. Bump even got himself a new pair of shoes.

Uncle Nemo could call the turkeys from the side of a hill. Crouched down in a blind, he'd hold his lips to his cupped hand, with a couple of fingers sticking straight up into the air. Gobble-gobble-gobble-gobble, he'd say.

Gobble-gobble-gobble-gobble, a turkey would answer back, from way down in the valley. The dance was on.

Nemo would allow a discreet silence, then call again, kind of nonchalantly this time, but with just a bit of jest in each gobble, like two potential lovers, alert and slightly aroused, aware of the pleasure of this particular quest. It always amazes me how quickly love can manifest itself, and in the most unexpected places, he'd say to me. You got to have good instincts when it comes to attraction, especially if it's going to be a hit-and-run.

Nephew, it's a mating call, he'd continue. You're telling the turkey that there's some lovin' up here. Come and get it. Yeeow! he'd holler, cocking his big woolly head all the way back on his shoulders and laughing real good, his eyes shining as they did only at the thought of death and sex. With turkey hunting, he had both at once. Sex and death. Maybe that's why he loved it so much.

He *always* got that turkey. We'd eat one every year at Christmas dinner, Up the Hill at Big Mom's.

Nemo also taught us how to go fishing, me and Greg, when we were boys. He'd drop us off at Bonner's Pond, get us started on the day's fun, then he'd go off for the day's work, fly-fishing the nearby creeks and streams, all day long without a break. Water's got to move for trout to be in it. The hot summer sun would have to come down before we'd see him again. He'd leave us a picnic lunch and thermoses of water and iced tea. Then he'd go off to find a place of his own. Which was infinitely better than fishing along his side, because you'd get exhausted, hot, tired, and start thinking about how very much you wanted to be elsewhere.

I love the feel of a fish when it hits your bait. Thump. That's what the feel would sound like: Thump. He's on. And then the art of reeling him in: giving a little string so that he can take the bait, but keeping the line fairly taut, so you're always in control. Reel it in, then hold back a bit. Reel it in, then hold a bit. Reel; hold. Reel. Hold.

Reel. You got a good one, nephew. Often, Nemo would net it out of the water for you. He took as much pleasure in our triumphs as in his own.

I enjoyed fishing and Uncle Jim's company most when I was a college student. I'd drive home from New Haven, eat one of Mama's favorite meals, go Up the Hill to see Big Mom, then fix a day and time to fish with Uncle Jim. It was always 5:00 a.m. or 5:30. And I'd be there, if barely awake. He'd toot the horn twice and sit in his truck at the bottom of our stairs on Hampshire Street. I'd drag out of bed and down the steps, and off we'd go to get Mr. Bump.

Bump Saville lived in a trailer court, just outside Keyser. We'd drag his boat and hitch it up, then we'd get coffee and doughnuts, which the three of us would share in the cab of Nemo's truck.

Five o'clock is not a time for a whole lot of talking. We'd talk later, in the boat. We always went to the same fishing hole, and we'd always stop to ask permission of the lady of the house, whom we'd always wake up. Good to see you too, Mr. Coleman. . . . You know you don't have to ask, and her voice would trail off. Nemo just liked to chat with that pretty woman, to see if she might need some of his sound advice and wise counsel about her tomatoes and corn, or, once, about nursing that little fawn they were keeping in the house until it got big enough, since its mother had been run down by wild dogs. The woman had started to nurse the fawn, using a pink baby bottle with a tan nipple, to keep it alive. Nemo's stare would have remained frozen all morning, at the sight of this woman in her nightshirt, feeding this suckling fawn. Shoot, Jim, Bump said. Them fish'll be chased away by the morning sun if we don't get on down to the dam. I couldn't help but remember the time that Aunt Helen's next-door neighbor, Lizzy, pulled her breast out of her blouse to nurse her baby in front of some preacher. I just happened to be there, visiting her older son. I had never seen a baby nurse before. That preacher stopped chewing to stare more fully. I gazed at the baby, the breast, and the bug-eyed preacher. That baby's hungry, he said. Yes, it is. That baby needs to be fed. His eyes bulged just like Nemo's.

They'd seat me first, so my feet stayed dry, then push us

off from the water's edge. The fog would cover the entire lake, so we'd be sailing blind. As the sun started to come up, the mist would burn off. The fish would hit as soon as we got into the water, lining up to the hooks of death. We'd hit so many in each separate hole, that we'd move around for variety. There was one old-timer that Nemo had hooked once but that got away. Nemo always looked out for him, and he, no doubt, for Nemo. Neither one wanted things any other way. I wonder if that fish knows that Nemo is dead.

We'd talk about things. Before you'd know it, the sun would be moving high overhead, the mist completely burned off. Not too hot, yet, to fish; but a good time to talk. We'd sit and cast, snap and reel, talking about whatever Nemo and Mr. Bump cared to talk about. Like religion or the End of the World or Commanists.

You can't be a Christian and a Commanist, Nemo would say, Bump nodding at the obviousness of the sentence, like The world is round, or The earth is flat.

Course you can, I said once without thinking. Poland has a whole nation of them.

Uh-oh, I thought, as the silence resounded. I figured that this was *it*. I never lied to Uncle Jim or Mr. Bump, but I did try to put things in such a way that they could climb inside what I had said. Mostly I listened and laughed with them. They liked to make me laugh, though what they were saying about Jesus and Commanists was no laughing matter.

Oh, Nemo finally responded. You mean *Catholic* Christians! Catholics ain't a *real* religion . . . just like your daddy's religion.

Now, Nemo wasn't "talking" about my Daddy, like you do when you signify or play the dozens. He was just making a considered observation, based on his considerable experience as a Minister of the Gospels, Sanctified Holiness Erin Street Baptist Church. The church had been empty since Reverend

Berry had died, when I was a boy, so Nemo and a brother or two had fixed it up and installed a new congregation. Nemo had been a sidekick to Mr. Les and then to Reverend Monk, but none of them really got along. It had been Monk who told him how to get his license. Twenty-five bucks and a postage stamp. The Lord will do the rest.

He had wanted his own church. And he got it. That's why he was Baptist and Sanctified: the building had been consecrated Baptist, the mail-order license said Sanctified. Nemo was a practical man.

He loved the mystery of the rites. The Body of Christ meant the *body* of Christ. You didn't want to take Communion every day; it spoiled it somehow. Made it too familiar for it to remain mysterious. First you wash the feet, then you eat the bread. And then you sip the grape juice. Jesus never drank wine. It was unfermented wine. That's one reason your daddy's church ain't a church. They can do anything in that place. That ain't a church. God don't like ugly. Not everybody who calls out the name Lord, Lord, shall enter the Kingdom of Heaven, Nephew. He had called me Nephew ever since I was a Cub Scout in his troop. I liked the way it sounded, the way it made me feel.

Uncle Jim was determined to enjoy the Gifts of the Spirit: wisdom, knowledge, prophecy, faith, healing the sick, the discerning of the spirit, and even miracles. But most of all, speaking in and interpretation of tongues.

He'd talk in tongues all day long, sounding like some Indian in a B movie on TV. Hey-yah-ho-o-o, yah . . . hey-yah-ho-o-o, yah, yah. Who you talking to, Uncle Jim? I'd ask, to be devilish, though only once in a great while, so as not to spoil the effect. Just talking to the Lord, son—just talking to the Lord.

If the Lord ever answered that nigger back, Daddy was fond of saying, he'd have a heart attack. Daddy's eyes would sparkle as he visualized Nemo's terror. Daddy said he always wanted to tie a microphone to the large rhododendron bush in our backyard and then, as Nemo walked by, get Charlton Heston to speak the way God did to Moses on Mount Sinai. (Sort of like I had done the day I hid under Daddy's bed, waited till he had gone to sleep, then intoned in the deepest voice I could muster at age seven: "Henry . . . Henry . . . This is your conscience . . . Buy that boy a Polaroid camera!")

Since God in His Infinite Wisdom had not granted Uncle Jim his fondest wish, all the Gifts of the Spirit, He must have had an alternate plan: He would give a different one to each of Nemo's daughters, and to friends or relatives, to the amount of seven. So Kay could prophesy, Roberta could heal, and all of them could speak in tongues, even Earkie. When Nemo surprised everybody and went to his Great Reward, Earkie took over, the Chosen Successor. The entire congregation was just about all family, especially Uncle Jim's children and theirs. Daddy called it Nemo Baptist Church. The Church of the Nemonites.

Uncle Jim had a way with festivities. Christmas at Uncle Jim's house boasted the biggest tree in the world, a train, a village mounted on a big wooden platform, artificial snow, and smoke pellets. Looked like Bavaria looks, down at Warner's Authentic German Restaurant. He always overdid it and was always borrowing money on the sly from Mr. Toots in December, when the credit union turned him down. Toots sympathized with Nemo. They both had had lots of women and lots of trouble.

But Nemo's true claim to fame was cooking the corn at the colored mill picnic. (The mill's segregated white picnic was held at a site safely ten miles away.) When they write the True History of the Valley and establish its Hall of Fame, they may recall ole Nemo for a lot of things, but there's no doubt that he'll be remembered as the champion chef of corn.

We'd get over to Carskadon's Farm at about seven. The men would build the picnic tables, two sets of two-by-fours nailed to two pairs of trees. The pine was clean and new; I loved its just-sawed smell. Nearby, a huge black cast-iron vat sat on two sets of cinder blocks, with pinewood in a pyre beneath. Zinc-galvanized milk containers full of water were stationed in a half circle around the vat: water for the corn. On the appointed hour, which only he knew, Uncle Jim would light the fire. Hours later, when the water came to a rolling boil, he'd dump in the red-net bushel bags of corn, picked that day. While we waited, we'd sip his coffee, mine rich and sweet with warm cream separated out for the occasion at the barn just over the hill.

The men would gossip to pass the time, savoring the thought of that corn. As they would talk, and the water would cook, the cars of the colored would start to come. Every family had its own spot, claimed for years and years, and newcomers parked way down at the far end of the field, near to where the gamblers congregated. Nobody messed with tradition at the mill picnic. No need to.

Colored people would come from miles around. There were Cadillacs and Lincolns, all clean and shiny like new. Sometimes rented for the occasion, so people would know they had done well leaving the Valley. From Cincinnati and Pittsburgh, Youngstown and Philadelphia, Dee-troit and "Chi," some even from as far west as California and as far north as Buffalo. Rochester was a popular spot, because of the Kodak plant there. Yonkers too. We were having none of that city-nigger stuff, though. The aristocracy lived in Piedmont, and the proof was this segregated picnic sponsored by the mill, to which all the dispersed flew back each year, as swallows did to Capistrano.

The mill finally shut it down, though, in 1970. Too segregated, they said. Against the law, they said. Between the closing of the high school, which meant the end of the town's basketball team, and the demise of the mill pic-a-nic, the town just about died, though nobody had the heart to tell it so.

I don't think that Uncle Jim tempted fate very often, and I don't think he was mean. But I do believe that he made a tragic mistake by not calling Mama and the rest of the tribe when he knew that Big Mom, finally, was about to die. Instead, he called a white preacher friend, Mr. Bob Harmon, a decision that nobody ever understood or forgave. Especially not Mama. I have my own theory about why he did it. I think he wanted to raise Big Mom from the dead, so only the truly faithful could be standing by. I never asked him, of course. But it was a laboratory right there on the sofa, where Biggie was dying, a once-in-a-lifetime chance to test his faith in God, and God's in him.

All that came of it was that there were more pissed-off niggers at that funeral than I had ever seen before or hope ever to see again. "The Lord told me who to call, and who not to call," was all he said. Which pissed them off even more. Them coons loved Miss Maggie, and no one wanted to let her go, least of all Miss Maggie herself, not even at the ripe old age of ninety-two.

I wrote the eulogy for her funeral, and Rocky read it at the service. Let her go, was my refrain; we've had her long enough. Let her go. Be thankful for the life she's lived, and our time together, and all the things she did that made life special. I never mentioned Heaven, or being at home with the Lord, or walking on Gold Pavements, or living in the House with Many Mansions.

I never mentioned them though I knew what the Colemans have on their minds when they think about religion and God. They imagine the afterlife as a deluxe Family Reunion at

Biggie's on Christmas, with the women serving the men and returning out to the kitchen with Big Mom, and Daddy Paul at the head of the table Up the Hill, struggling to remember a couple hundred grandchildren's names. Fried chicken everywhere, and one of Nemo's wild turkeys, the kind where the skin stays crisp, especially around the darkest meat. Sweet pickles, olives, and celery on the side, of course. And a limitless supply of iced tea, with plenty of ice cubes to pass around—rattle, rattle, rattle. Sweetened while it was hot, so that the sugar dissolved real good. A football game at the end of the day.

When Rocky finished, old Minister Bob Harmon leapt up, his face flushed, spitting his words. He had noticed the omission and disapproved. Yes, yes, he stammered and sputtered, but let's be thankful she's with the Lord, *right now*, this minute, up in Heaven with *Gawd-dah*. Meeting Daddy Paul and baby Gracie, singing spirituals and learning to flap her wings. Hallelujah!

I didn't know whether to laugh or cry. I just looked at the Gateses instead. I did it because we always knew when the break had come, always entered critical awareness together, a lockstep of the spirit, even me. That's what they specialized in: analyzing things when they were over, breaking things down one by one. Second-order consciousness. Metamouthing. Scrutinizing. Reading the signs. Expliciting the implicit. It was healing to do this.

Mama was still pissed off that Uncle Jim had not called her to help Big Mom die. He's next, she said grimly. And she was right, though she herself would not be long to follow.

Uncle Jim might have talked a lot about going to Heaven, and he definitely believed in the Devil and in Hell, but he was not anxious to cross over to the Other Side. Neither, as I said, was Big Mom, who met the Grim Reaper with both arms swinging. Nemo didn't even have a chance to be scared, which makes me think that God was merciful to him; that maybe He appreciated all that church-making, even if Nemo did push things a bit. He just wanted it all to work, wanted signs from God that everything was working, and he wanted it *today*. I'm hard on the Lord, he told me several times, with the greatest self-insight I'd ever seen him display.

As near as we can reconstruct things, Nemo was down Cumberland, at the clinic where a friend's daughter went to get her counseling. He had been very concerned about her going to jail for accidentally taking welfare checks from the government while she had a job. He had called me long-distance to say that there was something he wanted to talk about. I just figured he wanted a donation for his church and was prepared to give him something. No, he had been worried about this woman going to jail and how she couldn't take that. Would it all be OK?

So that's what he was fretting about when, they said, he just sat down and died. Like a thief in the night, he had always said. The Angel of Death had tapped his shoulder and lifted him right away. Boom—no warning. Boom—no time for fear, for spiritual preparation. His year was 1986. I *guess* he's in Heaven, if there is one, Pop sometimes says. I guess.

The trout and the deer were unable to attend the wake and didn't send a representative to the funeral.

When I learned of his death, I tried to imagine him in his state of rest.

But other images crowded my mind.

Like the way Nemo would fling those boiling husks of just-cut "carn" onto those makeshift pine tables, and the Negroes from way down at the end of the arc of parked cars, and the Negroes with seniority and clout, who could park right next to the boiling vat and the Kool-Aid and the ponies-for-riding and the tables set up for the watermelon contests, would be right by them, waiting for that corn to hit the pine, waiting for the boiling-hot water to splatter onto the ground and the trees and the strangers dumb enough to risk getting scalded or too stupid not to think of the heat, and then they'd hit those ears of corn like pigs on slop, pushing and shoving and elbowing their way to the center of the table, tossing those too-hot-to-handle ears back and forth between burning palms, until the palms got numb or the corn husks cooled, and then the real work'd begin. They'd rip the husk right down the corn, tossing the silk aside but leaving the husk to hang like an unbuttoned shirt still secured by your trousers. They'd dip brand-new paintbrushes, bought just for this purpose, in mason jars full of butter, slapping those steaming ears like latex or semigloss—slap-slap-slap, slap-slap-slap—sounding the butter. And then, ripping a shaker of salt from someone else, they'd douse the drowned ear with just about enough salt for a lifetime—slap-slap-slap, slap-slap-slap. Enough for everybody, enough for everybody, you could hear Old Nemo shout, if your presence of mind had not left for the chase. More out in fifteen minutes. Yee-ow! Fifteen minutes, there'll be more comin'. Nemo the Chef, Nemo Healer of the Sick, Raiser of the Dead, Nemo the Huntsman, Nemo the Trainmaster! Someone in this church has a headache, and the Lord wants that headache cured! Nemo the talker in tongues. Yee-ow! I used to sin that way! Yee-ow! Before I was saved . . . before I met the Holy Ghost. *Just talking to the Lord, son. Just talking to the Lord.*

15 / Shattering
the Sugar Bowl

W hen I started to grow up—to erupt, really—in the sixties, Daddy would let me listen to the men talk, in bars and in Mr. Comby Carroll's barbershop in Keyser. (I used to think his name was Comby Kurl, because that's how everybody in the Valley always said it. What an appropriate name, I thought, for a barber.) His real name was Nicomus Carroll, and he had one arm. Or rather, he had one good arm and one dead arm, which looked like one of those pink-to-slightly-purple pieces of pork that hang lengthwise in butchershops.

People say that God compensates a person when He takes away a sense or a limb. So a one-armed man has the strength of two arms in one, a blind man can hear like a deer and smell like a fox. And so forth. Now, I don't know if this sort of thing is true, but in Mr. Comby Kurl's case, his compensatory gift was the capacity to tell lies—an extraordinary capacity, in his case. Funny lies, too. That nigger could lie his ass off. Albert Lyin'stein, they called him.

Grown men, and boys, would crowd into his barbershop in Keyser, fifteen or twenty at a time, and sit there on Saturdays, patiently waiting their turn, listening to this man tell lies. All day long. Mr. Comby knew everybody's business, and everybody knew his. Except he didn't talk about that. Then again, why would he have to? He was sleeping with the nice lady who lived in the nice house that stood in back of the barbershop, maybe twenty or so yards away. After a riveting morning of lies, rumor, and gossip, just about the time he was in midstride, he'd announce abruptly that he was hungry, even if he had cut half of a person's head or had lathered a face up real good—and what could you possibly do? Then he'd disappear to consume his lunch. I think that the older men enjoyed the idea of sitting there in silence, turning ever so slowly the pages of the dirty magazines, thinking about ole Nicomus and wondering how long it would take Mr. Comby to eat his lunch.

Now, no one minded a person eating his lunch. It was dessert that took Mr. Comby a bit too long to devour. And dessert, every colored person in Mineral, Grant, and Hardy counties knew, was that nice colored lady who lived out in back of Mr. Comby's barbershop.

Damn lunch was *good* today, Mr. Comby would say an hour or so later, when he'd reappear, not one strand of his good hair out of place. Some days, if not too many people were around, or if he was feeling tender about things, he'd make a joke about paying his rent, or sitting on the radiator drying his lease, or depositing an insurance payment on the mortgage—something like that.

He'd stand at the barber chair all morning long, telling the dirtiest, funniest jokes, passing around girlie magazines that you've never heard of. I say the jokes were funny, but I'm not sure they were, because mostly I didn't understand them. Later, I'd sometimes ask my cousin Greg what such and such had meant. Greg, a year my senior, would always say, after the greatest deliberation: "To tell the truth, Skippy, I don't know myself." Sometimes he'd speculate before he said that, rubbing his chin and roaming freely among several equally untenable and absurd possibilities.

What color is come? I remember asking one day. Some say it's yellow, Greg said, some say it's white. I've even heard some say it's crystal clear. But to tell you the truth, Skippy, I don't know. I must have asked Greg a million questions about sex when I was nine or ten.

Sex education class for us was taught by Professor Nicomus Carroll. If you had started coming to the barbershop as a boy, you knew that the fellows had begun to think of you as a young man when Mr. Comby handed you one of his dirty magazines. It happened when you were lathered up in the chair for a manly "Washington Square" straight-razor trim along the back of your neck—which made me break out in razor bumps, no matter what I did—or when you were sitting in one of his beat-up, tattered chairs of tubular aluminum with red vinyl seats, battling to keep your feet warm in the winter or from going to sleep in the summer. For years, I had looked at *Ebony* or *Jet*, embarrassed by even the covers of the dirty magazines. Then it happened, or rather, two things happened, almost at once: Comby stopped giving me a sugar bowl haircut, and he let me look at a girlie magazine. I had come of age.

For me? I thought, as he placed the mag in my lap. "Look at how high her box is. Ain't that something?" he said to me. "Sure is," I mumbled. Box . . . I had better check with Greg to find out what a box is. I scanned the page thoroughly, to make sure I had seen the box, because Mr. Comby was examining me as I examined that high box. That box, for all I knew, could have been constructed out of cardboard and held fruit or tissue paper.

In the end, my cousin Greg, that encyclopedia of the world's arcane knowledge, confessed after a long pause: To tell you the truth, Skippy, I don't really *know* what a box is.

I still don't know exactly what Comby meant, because the picture was a centerfold of a woman in a bathing suit, the sort that still occupies the middle two pages of *Jet*. And while I did my best, I just didn't know what I was looking for. Besides, I thought she was not very pretty, which didn't help things.

Not getting a sugar bowl haircut was even more important than graduating from *Ebony* and *Jet* to *Penthouse* and *Playboy*. The haircut was so named for the unpoetic reason that, once upon a time, a "barber" placed a sugar bowl on your nappy head, then shaved your hair in a circle just below the bowl's edge. What genius of the tonsorial arts thought of this particular mode of torture, history does not record for us. But it separated the men from the boys. As a boy, I'd look wistfully at the men, and the adolescents, all lathered up, awaiting the straight-edge razor to make that perfectly continuous and clean line at the border where follicles end and neckline begins. Slowly, carefully, scrape, scrape, scrape. It looked good . . . till the next morning, when the scratch of a persistent itch revealed a line of raised razor bumps, the price one had to pay for the shattering of the sugar bowl.

I always felt a certain warmth in Mr. Comby Carroll's barbershop and didn't mind the long wait for a cut. The stories were so funny, and often people would talk about the news or current events, and I did know something about that. I was a tape recorder, incising on my memory anything that came along. But most of all, I liked to watch the men laugh. And that they did all day long, especially when discussing who was doing what to whom in the sanctity of the bedroom—or, more likely, in the back seat of a car, up on Radical Hill, in the colored cemetery, down to Keyser.

One of the chief chroniclers of the town's nocturnal exploits was Roebuck Johnson, who was about six feet tall, lanky but muscular, a coffee-colored man with short hair and a well-trimmed mustache. The men said that Roebuck had the biggest dick in Piedmont. I don't know about that. But he had two full-time lovers for twenty-five years, plus a wife and five children, and he could drink Scotch whiskey over crushed ice in water glasses all afternoon at the VFW. I guess he was a needy man. On the subject of the exploits of others, his reserves of information and speculation seemed inexhaustible.

One day, I heard Daddy and Roebuck do a genealogy of my friends' and neighbors' proper and unlawful parentage, house to house, row by row, from Water and Paxton streets on Back Street, to Erin Street and Rat Tail Road up on the Hill. I was devastated. It seemed that virtually *nobody's* daddy was his daddy, and everybody in town (except me, apparently) knew. There were exceptions, of course: Roebuck's kids and Daddy's belonged to them, they claimed. But if they were right, the genetic chaos strewn by the sexual mores of the colored people of Piedmont would be enough to drive the director of research at the Mormon Genealogical Institute berserk. And the truth of their claims, as usual, was clinched once they pointed out the family resemblances between fathers and their putative stray children.

No! I said, over and over again, laughing out loud but really quite shocked. Look at that boy! Roebuck or Pop would respond. Who does he look like? Devastating evidence, I'd think. Irrefutable. Conclusive. Good as a DNA test. It seemed my uncles had stray children, my father's friends and fellow workers had stray children, all of our neighbors had stray children. It was astonishing. My whole idea of the family unit had shifted latterly, door to door. People in Piedmont didn't have family trees; they had hedges and shrubbery, running long and wide. And Mr. Johnson was the president of the Genealogical Society of Potomac Valley, because he was the chief spewer of genes.

What's more, the oddest people were held to be the greatest lovers. Mr. Bootsie was a pear-shaped yellow man, with slicked-back straight hair and uneven yellow teeth, who chain-smoked cigars. He was also a terrible driver, who rode his clutch up and down the Piedmont hills. And that ain't all he rode, I was assured. He worked at the paper mill, as did most everybody else, on the platform with the loaders, just like every other colored man did who wanted to work at the mill. But Bootsie had money to spend, apparently—"what with being single and all," as my daddy liked to say, a mite wistfully.

Mr. Bootsie used to take up collection at church—Big Mom's church, Walden Methodist—and he picked up the weekly pledges or tithes that you would put in an envelope and donate outside of collection. Evidently, he was a real good collector. The best. Young girls, old girls, middle-aged girls, Roebuck would say, Bootsie collects them all.

His two regular women were Miss Ezelle and Miss Mabel. Miss Ezelle is beautiful *now*, at seventy-plus, so she must have been ravishing back then, in the 1940s. She and her husband had been married just a little while. He was a very tall, very gentle, light-complected man, with kind of a red tinge to his skin, and rusty-sandy hair. His lips were especially pinkish-red, and his lower lip pouted a bit. On Saturday nights or Sundays at church, he was *sharp*: like Uncle Joe, he wore those see-through ribbed silk socks, always black or dark gray. And a hat. He liked to dance and was a good dancer. But he drank too much, and too often. And when he drank, he became sad and would tell you over and over how much he loved Miss Ezelle, and then he'd start to cry.

He should stop drinking, I said to my parents one day. And they just said uh-huh and kept on doing what they were doing, moved right along to another subject.

What I didn't yet know was that according to the town,

Miss Ezelle went to see Mr. Bootsie one day and proposed a business arrangement: her favors in return for his cash. Seems everybody knew it. Including her husband. Miss Ezelle was always "clean," as we say, well dressed and well groomed. Almost as smart-looking as Mama. Keeps herself nice, people in Piedmont say about someone who attends closely to her looks. So they had an affair of sorts, a business affair, from shortly after her marriage in the 1940s clean up to the time Mr. Bootsie died, just a few years ago. Everybody knew; nobody minded. Nobody, that is, but her husband.

He liked Daddy and respected my mom. Everybody respected Mama, except her sister, Aunt Marguerite, who was mad at her all the time because, for reasons that remain obscure, Mama was mad at her all the time. As gracious, and as refined, and as generous as she could be, my mama could hate unalterably. And she thrilled at the idea of vengeance.

Mama liked Miss Ezelle's husband, though. And she liked Miss Ezelle too. Everybody did. There was no violence between her two men, not even harsh words. And no harsh words in town about Miss Ezelle, which is curious, for the colored people in Piedmont could wag some hellacious tongues. In bitterly jealous rivalries at the Labor Day dances held by the colored American Legion in Keyser, the Legion named in honor of the two Stewart boys (not related) who died during the war, issues were fought out with knives or razors or hands. But not around Miss Ezelle. Her husband's violence was directed at himself, and he drowned the complexity of his situation in a sea of whiskey. "Just hold my head back for me," he once cried out to Daddy, "and pour it in."

When I was an adult living Elsewhere, and home for the holidays, I once saw him fall *up* the steps, the steps leading up from our backyard, connecting the end of our property on East Hampshire Street (where we'd moved in 1977) with Erin Street, running parallel just above.

It was Christmas Day, and on Christmas Day everybody

visits everybody, to look at people's trees, to see the best thing that Santa Claus brought them, to sample the goodies out of their kitchens, but especially to take a nip. Even after Daddy had stopped drinking, which was about the time I was born, he always had "a bottle" on hand on Christmas Day and would offer it generously, even to his already drunken friends.

Miss Ezelle's husband was drunk, of course, as he almost always was. He'd stayed a very long time and seemed to be having a very good time. Stumbling up our back path, knee-deep in snow, arm in arm with a drinking buddy, he tripped and fell and lay prone in the snow, unconscious. When he came to, he swore off alcohol, and he stayed sober, I hear, ever since.

Mr. Bootsie also loved Miss Mabel, and *this* was the "case" that people perplexed about whenever they got around to talking about these things. Bootsie would go visit her husband, Mr. Jingles, and give him some of his always bountiful cash, or take him a bottle. Mr. Jingles would spend the cash on a bottle, or drink the one that Mr. Bootsie would bring to him, while Bootsie would go on upstairs and diddle Miss Mabel. "That's the real stopper," Uncle Joe once said to Daddy. "I ain't never heard of such a thing." Neither have I. But Mabel and her husband apparently loved each other. They also loved Lady, a furry black-and-white dog with stubby legs and a long back, who seemed as intelligent as half the kids I knew. They were the first colored people I knew who kept their dog in the house, like a person.

Years later, when I was home from college, Roebuck Johnson told me an oddly personal story: that's when I knew that he thought of me as "a man," and that Daddy did too. He said he had just made love to his woman, and when she went to the bathroom to wash, he sneaked a phone call to his other woman, just to say he loved her, did she love him, and see you tomorrow. Why, did I think, would a man do that?

He'd do that, I said—college kid that I was—to protect

himself from being vulnerable to the woman in the bathroom, from caring so much that he could be hurt, or become desperate or crazy. And so he'd keep that distance in his mind he needed to stay aloof, to retain control. And yes, it meant he *was* crazy.

That's what the barbershop Sigmund Freud rattled off. But the truth is, I was astonished by Mr. Johnson's story. It occurred to me that he was making his grand confession because he saw in me his son Roebuck, Jr., who had been my classmate and close friend, saw it as a way of explaining himself to his son. All those years of public infidelity. All those years of projecting infidelity onto his wife. She was loyal to the end— Roebuck's end—which was the problem. He died not long after his lover did. But as flattered as I was that Roebuck was talking to me like a man, I discovered that I was not all that eager to be invited into too much intimacy with an adult. Being a child had its advantages. I wanted to slow things down just a bit.

16 / Abandoning Ship

At sixteen, I became one of the founding members of the Fearsome Foursome, a group consisting of Roland Fisher (called Ben or Fisher), Jerry Price (Roy's oldest son, who looked just like him and was known as "Soul Moe"), Rodney Galloway (called Swano, or Swineo, depending on how nasty someone was trying to be), and me. Moe and Fisher called me Gates, or Goops Man; Swano, for obscure reasons, called me the Professor.

At Peterkin, I had experienced the sort of social intimacy and easy camaraderie with whites that I had known in Piedmont in elementary school, but that had started to wane the older we got. When it was no longer available, I just gave up, socially, on white kids, the kind I knew from home, anyway. Linda was deep into a relationship with a white boy from Keyser Road, who was not exactly a brain. But he loved the woods, and that's where they spent their time together, making love, I imagined. Dip was crazy in love with a girl who had had a baby by somebody else. He was being initiated into the soft and wet pleasures of the flesh. You could see his whole demeanor change, the worldly knowledge he started to wear

181

on his face. I envied him that knowledge. He never bragged about what they were doing together. I remember being astonished at that, at how quiet he was about their passion. He hadn't been quiet about anything else; none of us had. Quiet was not our mode, especially about the sex we had never had. But Dip was having sex. At least it looked that way to me.

My fellow Fearsomes were all on the basketball team, so I learned how to keep the statistics. We did just about everything together, in Fisher's brother's dilapidated car, a 1959 Chrysler, purple, with big tail fins and a push-button convertible top. Fisher used black masking tape to keep it from leaking. We named it the Soul Mobile, and we used it to cruise. Down to Keyser, down the length of Main Street, up New Creek, to the bowling alley and Jimmy's Pizza Shop, back to Piedmont, across the bridge to Westernport and Teen Town, back to Keyser, and then ending at my house. By this time, we lived on Erin Street, in what was a big house for us; Rocky and I even had our own rooms. There was plenty of good food, a big TV, and a stereo in my room. They loved coming to my house.

I joined Record Club of America so I could get the latest soul albums but also get into jazz, which I began to learn about in *Ebony* and in the books about black people I was reading. I was already deep into rhythm and blues, which became "soul" in 1965 or so. Jimmy and David Ruffin were solid, reliable favorites. Lou Rawls's *Live* album was our bridge backward (in time) to the blues and forward in time to jazz. I learned the names of the country's urban ghettos by memorizing his song "South Side Blues." Learning to listen to jazz was like stepping into a secret universe.

I'll never forget the day we first heard John Coltrane. I had read lots about his death at age forty and about what a genius he was. So I ordered *Expressions* from the catalogue listing, along with *History of Otis Redding* and *Aretha's Greatest*

Hits. After listening to Redding and Aretha Franklin, we dropped down *Expressions*. Stunned silence: then Soul Moe announced that the album had to be defective, so I should send it back and exchange it for Slim Harpo's *Baby, Scratch My Back*. I wanted to believe him, but I knew it wasn't true. That stuff is too deep for young boys, my uncle Earkie had said; too deep even for me. Soul Moe liked deep-down rhythm and blues: he kept *Randy's Record Shop* open. He didn't want me to listen to it too much, he'd say, because he wasn't sure I could handle all that soul.

About that time, I started to smoke. First a pipe, wadded with sweet, sickening Cherry Blend. And then Tareyton cigarettes. Both left me nauseated. I could smoke in my room and only my room, Mama and Daddy had said. I'd rather you do it here than sneak around, was Daddy's watchword. My room became my refuge.

One day, Uncle Raymond, next to last of the Coleman brothers, came stealthily up the steps, following the trail of smoke like Nemo hunting a deer. Caught you! he shouted like a crazy man, scaring me half to death. I'm through with you now, he kept repeating, I'm through with you now. I used to slip you five dollars once in a while, I used to let you drive my car, but I'm through with you now. Fuck you, then, I thought, walking over to the banister of our upstairs hallway and shouting after him: "If this makes you stop loving me, then you must not have loved me very much," and similar protestations. Black bastard, I thought. Not smoking or drinking was part of being a Coleman, and I was eager to do both.

But if Raymond had written me off as a delinquent, my relations with a few of the other Coleman brothers, including Earkie, were getting pretty rocky too. For them, my smoking was only a symbol of my waywardness. And their disapproval was reciprocated. If I felt I was through with the white people I knew at Piedmont, I was starting to figure I was through

with those Coleman coons too. Not all of them, you understand; and not my aunts, who loved me to pieces. But my
uncles and I did battle more and more, especially when I
stopped being a Negro, turned black, and grew the first Afro
in Piedmont, West Virginia. Don't you call him Mister, I'd
complain to Mama—he called you Pauline. Mama, defiant of
her brethren, would not censure my new style; I was her
baby, come what might. And the change in political climate
encouraged her to voice more freely (among family at least)
her long-nurtured hatred of white people.

Only later did I come to realize that for many of the colored
people in Piedmont—and for a lot of the older Colemans in
particular—integration was experienced as a loss. The warmth
and nurturance of the womblike colored world was slowly and
inevitably disappearing, in a process that really began on the
day they closed the door for the last time at Howard School,
back in 1956. Within our family, integration anxiety played
itself out broadly in terms of generations; those who had graduated from the colored high school found the adjustment
much harder than those who had gone only to the segregated
elementary school, if that. A principal focus of the resulting
tension was the raising of children—the issues of their rights
and responsibilities and their relation to authority, both white
and familial. I heard it times beyond counting: That boy's got
too much mouth. And from their perspective, my brother and
I probably did have too much mouth. Faced with what must
have been a painful choice between her loyalty to her brothers
and her loyalty to the sons whose independence she nurtured
and encouraged, my mother never wavered. Much to the
chagrin of the Coleman clan, she always took our side.

Clearly, the way she raised her children was perceived by
them as a threat: it represented chaos, disrespect for tradition,
order, containment. And it was reckless—insufficiently heed-
ful of the fact that the white world could crush us all anytime

it wanted to. Because I flouted the rules, they thought I would come to a bad end, and they took pleasure in letting me know that. Deep down, I think they were frightened for me. And deeper down, I think I frightened them.

Raymond could scarcely bear to set eyes on me. When are you going to get that nappy shit cut? he'd ask me, looking balefully at my still tentative Afro. Boy, sometimes I wonder about you. He and his brothers called me alternately "Malcolm" and "Stokely," and did so with the purest derision.

The way I figured, they just didn't get it. Maybe most of the colored people in Piedmont still didn't. But my friends did. We were a black consciousness cultural club. We began to read books together, black books, and to discuss them— Claude Brown, Eldridge Cleaver, Ralph Ellison, and Malcolm X. I could order them through Red Bowls, pay for them with the money I got redeeming bottles.

Back in eighth grade, I had seen W. E. B. Du Bois's photograph in our history textbook, stuck near the end of the section on the twentieth century, like a black-and-white postage stamp. (We never got to the civil rights chapters in our textbooks.) "He's a Communist," was Daddy's contribution to black history. I couldn't wait to read him, though it wouldn't be till college.

Now, two years later, I did a book report for Mrs. Iverson on Dick Gregory's new autobiography, *Nigger*, and a battle of wills ensued: about her saying the title. She refused. I had said it first, but her awkwardness made the word sound dirty, even in my mouth. Most of all, I remember the funny shade of crimson Mrs. Iverson's face took on when the nurtured crescendo of my oral presentation somehow culminated on that word: *"nigger."* And I sat down to silence, part of me satisfied, part of me frightened, but all the time knowing I had passed through some kind of gate. Unlike the bottles I sold to Red, I was nonreturnable.

We'd just gone through the summer of 1966, the summer when Stokely Carmichael announced something he called "Black Power" and many of the Negroes became black people and grew big Afros and started wearing dashikis and beads. I got goose bumps just thinking about being *black*, being proud of being black and learning to look at bushed-up kinky hair and finding it beautiful. KKK hair, Daddy called it: Knotty, Kinky, and Kan't-comby.

To older generations, we must have looked like freaks in a carnival, walking around muttering the few Swahili phrases we had managed to memorize, giving each other complicated soul handshakes, and putting our clenched fists over our hearts and saying things like "my beautiful black brothers and sisters." And in some ways it seems funny to me now. But it was an exciting and sincere effort to forge a new communal identity among a people descended from splendid ancient cultures, abducted and forced into servility, and now deprived of collective economic and political power. We thought we had learned at last our unutterable, secret name, and that name was BLACK. We believed that if we uttered it again and again, like an incantation, we would move mountains just as surely as Ali Baba had done, or knock down barriers like Joshua, who fit the battle of Jericho and the walls came tumbling down.

This people who had spent a couple of hundred years ironing, frying, greasing, and burning their hair, doing everything but pulling it out by its roots in an attempt to make it unkinky, had all of a sudden become converts to a new religion, the Holy Order of the Natural Kink. It drew sharp divisions in our communities: B.C. and A.D.—Before Crinkle and After Da Straightener. An Afro looked like a crown of cultural glory on the right head. If you took care of your Afro, kept the split ends cut, and washed and combed it regularly, it could emerge like a radiant halo of blackness. Cotton candy of kinkiness. Bad hair was now "good," and lots of people with "good" hair—especially the guiltily light-complected—were busy trying to kink theirs up. The world had turned upside down. Light-complected people were attempting to become darker, to distance and deny their white ancestors, intruders in their genetic line. One-fifth Yoruba, one-fifth Ashanti, one-fifth Mandinka, one-fifth this, and one-fifth that . . .

Of course, our consciousness was still at a relatively early stage, with respect to the emerging creed of blackness, and there were other things to preoccupy the Fearsome Foursome. Most of all we had my daddy. My three friends had no relationships with their fathers. Roy was too busy drinking and carousing, Swano never did have a daddy, and Fisher's father, Mr. Ben, seemed aloof and distant. Roland and I were born in the same hospital, three days apart, and his father always said that he picked up the wrong baby. I would have been crushed under that burden.

So by the time I was sixteen, my buddies had adopted my daddy as their surrogate father, and the four of us would sit for hours arguing with Daddy and Mama, eating dinner, watching television, and arguing some more. Vietnam, Black Power, Dr. King, Stokely, Afros, the Panthers, the time of day. We'd fall asleep in my bedroom, the four of us, then get up and argue with the Old Man some more. We'd argue with Daddy for hours on end. You boys are *crazy*, he'd say when he wanted a break. You're as crazy as Skip. We'd watch the riots, watch the convention, watch the bombings, watch the entire news. We were close enough to D.C. that I could buy the *Washington Post* every day, so I read it during lunch at school and would share the results with the fellas.

We watched the war together, we watched the King assassination together, we watched Bobby Kennedy's assassination together. Daddy always had been a conspiracy buff; he hated Lynchin' Johnson, as he called him, and was convinced in November of 1963 that *he* had killed JFK.

The irony was, Daddy wasn't much more in sympathy with my new politics and hairstyle than the Colemans; yet the things that would divide me from the Colemans provided a point of contact for Daddy and me. For one thing, after years of ritual silence, even argument was an improvement. And arguing—a playful give-and-take—would prove the means by which we rebuilt our relationship, establishing a camaraderie broad enough to include my friends, as well.

For us, the Fearsome Foursome, part of discovering politics was trying to be political ourselves. The Fearsome organized the first school boycott in the history of Piedmont. All the black kids stayed home on the day of the King funeral—and got bad citizenship grades in return. Some of us attended prayer vigils, like the one we organized at the Episcopal church.

Not until my late teens did I learn that we weren't quite the pioneers of protest we imagined ourselves to be. It turned out that what was now the Holiness church was once the colored elementary school. Some years before I was born, Mama and practically the whole colored town led a civil rights march demanding the right of the colored to be educated, if only in their own schools. The way it had been, you went only to the eighth grade in the one-room school, then had to ride the bus to Cumberland to attend George Washington Carver School, which is where Daddy met Mama. But that the Coleman family, aside from Mama, was much involved in that protest was something I greatly doubted.

If Mama's tolerance separated her from her brethren, Daddy's intolerance, jocular though it was, separated him from his. Indeed, the other Gateses were positively approving toward me and my budding political ideas. You couldn't style an Afro with hair as good as theirs, but they were freethinkers and, as such, welcomed me into their ranks.

VI / One Day Next Tuesday

17 / Sin Boldly

In 1968, three of the Fearsome Foursome graduated from high school. Soul Moe was called upon to serve his country in Vietnam, and Swano and I would head down to Potomac State. (Roland had been held back a couple of years.) I gave the valedictory address at graduation, defying tradition by writing my own speech—surreptitiously, because this was not allowed. All through the last six weeks of marking period I had practiced delivering the traditional prepared speech with Miss Twigg, our senior English teacher, then had gone home to rehearse my real speech with Mama. Mama had a refined sense of vocal presentation and a wonderful sense of irony and timing. My speech was about Vietnam, abortion, and civil rights, about the sense of community our class shared, since so many of us had been together for twelve years, about the individual's rights and responsibilities in his or her community, and about the necessity to defy norms out of love. I searched the audience for Miss Twigg's face, just to see her expression when I read the speech! She turned as red as a beet, but she liked the speech, and as good as told me so with a big wink at the end of the ceremony.

My one year at Potomac State College of West Virginia University, in Keyser, all of five miles away, was memorable for two reasons: because of my English classes with Duke Anthony Whitmore and my first real love affair, with Maura Gibson.

I came to Potomac State to begin that long, arduous trek toward medical school. I enrolled in August 1968, a week before Labor Day, and I was scared to death. While I had been a good student at Piedmont High, I had no idea how well I would fare in the big-time competition of a college class that included several of the best students from Keyser High, as well as bright kids from throughout the state. I had never questioned my decision to attend Potomac State; it was inevitable: you went there after Piedmont High, as sure as the night follows the day. My uncles Raymond and David had attended it in the fifties, my brother in the early sixties, and my cousin Greg had begun the year before. I would attend too, then go off to "the university"—in Morgantown—to become a doctor.

Greg had told me about life on campus, about the freedom of choice, about card parties in the Union, and, of course, about the women. But he had also told me one thing early in his freshman year that had stayed with me throughout my senior year in Piedmont. "There's an English teacher down there," he had said, "who's going to blow your mind."

"What's his name?" I responded.

"Duke Anthony Whitmore," he replied.

"*Duke?*" I said. "What kind of name is Duke? Is he an Englishman?"

"No, dummy," Greg replied. "He's a white guy from Baltimore."

So as I nervously slouched my way through registration a year later, I found myself standing before the ferocious Mr. Gallagher, who enjoyed the reputation of being tough. He gave me the name of my adviser.

I looked at the name; it was not Whitmore. "Can I be assigned to Mr. Whitmore?" I ventured. "Because I've heard quite a lot about him from my cousin."

"You'll have to ask him," Mr. Gallagher said. "He's over there."

I made my way to Mr. Whitmore's table, introduced myself tentatively, stated my case, telling him my cousin Greg had said that he was a great teacher, a wonderful inspiration, etc., etc. What Greg had really said was: "This guy Whitmore is *crazy*, just like you!" It was love at first sight, at least for me. And that, in retrospect, was the beginning of the end of my twelve-year-old dream of becoming a doctor.

Learning English and American literature from the Duke was a game to which I looked forward every day. I had always loved English and had been blessed with some dedicated and able teachers. But reading books was something I had always thought of as a pastime, certainly not as a vocation. The Duke made the study of literature an alluring prospect.

Duke Whitmore did not suffer fools gladly. He did not suffer fools at all. Our classes—I enrolled in everything he taught, despite his protests, which I have to say weren't very strenuous—soon came to be dominated by three or four voices. We would argue and debate just about everything from Emerson and Thoreau to the war in Vietnam and racial discrimination. He would recite a passage from a poem or play, then demand that we tell him, rapid-fire, its source.

"*King Lear*," I responded one day.

"What act, what scene, Mr. Gates?" he demanded.

"Act Three, Scene Four," I shouted out blindly, not having the faintest clue as to whether the passage that he had recited was from *Hamlet* or the Book of Job.

"Exactly," he responded with a certain twinkle in his eye. "Sin boldly," he would tell me later, citing Martin Luther. My reckless citation was wrong, of course, but he wished to reward me for my audacity.

It was a glorious experience. Words and thoughts, ideas and visions, came alive for me in his classroom. It was he who showed me, by his example, that ideas had a life of their own and that there were other professions as stimulating and as rewarding as being a doctor.

After an academically successful year, Professor Whitmore encouraged me to transfer to the Ivy League. I wrote to Harvard, Yale, and Princeton. Since I had cousins who had gone to Harvard and Princeton, I decided to try for Yale. I sent off the application and took a summer job in the personnel office of the paper mill. I'd been hired for the express purpose of encouraging a few black people to transfer into the craft unions; I recruited them and administered the necessary tests. In three months, each union had been integrated, with barely an audible murmur from its members. Things were changing in Piedmont—a little.

Though we didn't become an item until our freshman year at Potomac State, Maura Gibson and I had known each other from a distance in high school. I used to run into her at the bowling alley and at Jimmy's Pizza next door. She was sharp on her feet and loved to argue. Once, she took me to task for talking about race so much. You can't talk about the weather without bringing up race, she charged. I was embarrassed about that at first, then pleased.

Once we were at college, Maura and I started having long talks on the phone, first about nothing at all and then about everything. The next thing I remember happening between us was parking in her green Dodge up in the colored cemetery on Radical Hill, near where just about all the Keyser colored, and much of the white trash, lived. "Radical" is a synonym in the valley for tacky or ramshackle. I'm not sure which came first, the name or what it came to mean. That's where we were when Horse Lowe (the coach of the college's football team and the owner of the property that abuts the colored cemetery) put his big red face into Maura's window, beat on the windshield with his fist, then told me to get the hell off his property.

Horse Lowe would wait until a couple had begun to pet heavily, then he'd sneak up on the car. He liked to catch you exposed. Even so, we used to park up there all the time. I figured that he'd get tired of throwing us out before I got tired of parking.

On weekends during the summer of 1969, I'd drive over to Rehoboth Beach, in Delaware, to see Maura, who was working as a waitress at a place called the Crab Pot. I'd leave work on Friday at about four o'clock, then drive all the way to Delaware, through Washington and the Beltway, past Baltimore and Annapolis, over the Chesapeake Bridge, past Ocean City, arriving at Rehoboth before midnight, with as much energy as if I had just awakened. We'd get a motel room after her shift ended, and she'd bring a bushel of crabs, steamed in the hot spice called Old Bay. We'd get lots of ice-cold Budweiser and we'd have a feast, listening to Junior Walker play his saxophone, play "What Does It Take" over and over and over again. "What does it take to win your love for me? . . ."

Since Maura was white, I felt that I was making some sort of vague political statement, especially in the wake of Sammy Davis, Jr., and *Guess Who's Coming to Dinner*. Others concurred. We were hassled at the beach. Somehow, for reasons having to do with nudity and sensuality, blacks were not allowed to walk along most beachfronts or attend resorts. I personally integrated many places at Rehoboth Beach that summer.

I was used to being stared at and somewhat used to being the only black person on the beach, or in a restaurant, or at a motel. But I hadn't quite realized how upset people could be until the day that some white guy sicced his Saint Bernard on me as Maura and I walked by. Certainly Maura and I had been no strangers to controversy, but we usually took pains not to invite it. Back home, we had sneaked around at first, hiding in cemeteries and in a crowd of friends, almost never being seen together in public alone. Until we were found out—by her father, of all people. A man called " 'Bama," of all things.

It was the evening we had agreed to meet at the big oak tree on Spring Street in Keyser, near one of her friends' houses. I picked her up in my '57 Chevrolet, and we went up to harass the Horse. Afterward, I dropped her off, then drove the five miles back to Piedmont. By the time I got home, Maura had called a dozen times. It turned out that her father had followed her down the street and hidden behind a tree while she waited, had watched her climb into my car. He knew the whole thing.

And he, no progressive on race matters, was sickened and outraged.

Soon, it seemed, all of the Valley knew the whole thing, and everybody had an opinion about it. We were apparently the first interracial couple in Mineral County, and there was hell to pay. People began making oblique threats, in the sort of whispers peculiar to small towns. When friends started warning my parents about them, they bought me a '69 Mustang so I could travel to and from school—and the colored graveyard—safely. (The Chevy had taken to conking out unpredictably.) Some kids at Potomac State started calling us names, anonymously, out of dormitory windows. And in the middle of all this chaos, 'Bama Gibson, Maura's father, decided he was going to run for mayor.

Lawd, Lawd, Lawd.

In his own redneck way, 'Bama Gibson was a perfectly nice man, but he was not exactly mayoral material. He had been a postman and became some sort of supervisor at the post office. He was very personable, everybody liked him, and he knew everybody's business, the way a postman in any small town does. With the whole town talking about how terrible it was that his daughter was dating a colored boy, and the men giving him their sympathy and declaring what they'd do to that nigger if that nigger ever touched their daughter, old 'Bama up and announced his candidacy.

Dr. Church, former president of the college, was the obvious front-runner. People were saying he'd already started to measure the mayor's office for new curtains. Certainly no one would have given 'Bama any hope of beating Dr. Church, even before my nappy head came on the horizon. With you on these crackers' minds, Daddy told me, he's got two chances: slim and none. Boy, how do you *get* into all this trouble?

Meantime, at the height of the campaign, Roland, Jerry, Swano, and I decided to integrate the Swordfish, a weekend hangout where all the college kids went to listen to a live band—usually E. G. Taylor and the Sounds of Soul, a white band with a black, Eugene Taylor, as lead singer. Eugene could *sing*. He wasn't so great with learning the words, but that Negro could warble. He'd make up words as he went along, using sounds similar to those he could not remember but making no sense.

Still, we wanted the right to hear Eugene mess up James Brown's words, same as anybody else, so we started to plot our move. Late one Friday night, when the Swordfish was rocking and packed, we headed up New Creek in our Soul Mobile, which we had washed for the occasion, even replacing the old masking tape over the holes in the roof. The Fearsome Foursome made their date with destiny. We were silent as we drove into the parking lot. There was nothing left to say. We were scared to death but just had to get on with it.

We parked the car and strolled up the stairs to the Swordfish. Since there was no cover charge, we walked straight into
the middle of the dance floor. That's when the slo-mo started,
an effect exacerbated by the strobe lights. Everybody froze:
the kids from Piedmont and Keyser who had grown up with
us; the students from Potomac State; the rednecks and crackers from up the hollers, the ones who came to town once a
week all dressed up in their Sears, Roebuck perma-pressed
drawers, their Thom McAn semi-leather shoes, their ulti-
mately *white* sox, and their hair slicked back and wet-looking.
The kids of rednecks, who liked to drink gallons of 3.2 beer,
threaten everybody within earshot, and puke all over themselves—they froze too, their worst nightmare staring them in
the face.

After what seemed like hours but was probably less than
a minute, a homely white boy with extra-greasy blond hair
recovered and began to shout "Niggers" as his face assumed
the ugly mask of hillbilly racism. I stared at this white boy's
face, which turned redder and redder as *he* turned into the
Devil, calling on his boys to kick our asses: calling us niggers
and niggers and niggers to help them summon up their courage. White boys started moving around us, forming a circle
around ours. Our good friends from Keyser and Potomac State
were still frozen, embarrassed that we were *in* there, that we
had violated their space, dared to cross the line. No help from
them. (I lost lots of friends that night.) Then, breaking through
the circle of rednecks, came the owner, who started screaming: Get out of here! Get out of here! and picked up Fisher
and slammed his head against the wall. It wasn't easy to see
because of all the smoke and because of the strobe effect of
the flashing blue lights, but I remember being surprised at
how Roland's Afro had kept its shape when his head sprang
back off the wall, the way a basketball keeps its shape no
matter how much or how hard you dribble it.

Moe and I hauled Fisher off the ground, with Swano's broad shoulders driving through the 'necks the way Bubba Smith used to do for the Baltimore Colts. I wondered if Roland's head would stop bleeding. Fuck you, motherfucker, I heard myself say. We're gonna shut your racist ass down. We're gonna shut your ass down, repeated Moe and Swano in chorus. Take a good look around you, you crackers, cuz this is your last time here.

We dragged Fisher to the car, ducking the bottles and cans as we sped away. Roland's head had stopped its bleeding by the time we passed Potomac Valley Hospital, which we called the meat factory because one of the doctors was reputed to be such a butcher, so we drove on past it and headed for my house. What'll y'all do now? Daddy asked as Mama bandaged Roland Fisher's head.

And yes, the place was shut down. We called the State Human Rights Commission on Monday, and the commissioner, Carl Glass, came up to Piedmont a few days later. He interviewed the four of us separately, and then he went out to the Swordfish and interviewed the proprietor, who by this time had told everybody white and colored in Keyser that he was going to get that troublemaker Gates. He swore to the commissioner that he would close down before he let niggers in. The commissioner took him at his word and sent an official edict telling him to integrate or shut down. As the man promised, he shut it down. And that is why the Swordfish nightclub is now Samson's Family Restaurant, run by a very nice Filipino family.

Well, all of this broke out in the middle of 'Bama Gibson's campaign to be the first postman elected as Mayor of Keyser, West Virginia, The Friendliest City in the U.S.A., as the road sign boasted—to which we chorused "bullshit" whenever we passed it.

The whole town talked about this campaign, from sunup to

sundown. And there were some curious developments. Our family doctor, Dr. Staggers (our high school principal, Mr. Staggers's son), went out of his way to tell me that lots of his friends, well-educated and liberal, had decided to suspend disbelief and vote for 'Bama, just to prove (as he put it) that Keyser is not Birmingham. Then the colored people, who never voted, decided to register and turn out for good ole 'Bama. The college kids at Potomac State, the ones not busy calling Maura "nigger-lover" from their dormitory windows, turned out in droves. And all the romantics who lived in Keyser, those who truly respected the idea of love and passion, voted for 'Bama. All both of them. Bizarrely enough, the election was turning into a plebiscite on interracial relationships.

I stayed out of Keyser on the day of the election, terrified that I'd already caused Maura's father to lose. If it's close, there's no sense aggravating the ones sitting on the fence, rubbing their nose in it, Daddy had said. And so I waited for Maura's phone call, which came around eleven-thirty and informed me that we had nothing more to worry about, her father had trampled Dr. Church. No longer would the police follow us, daring us to go even one mile over the speed limit. That's what she told me, and I could scarcely believe it. I started parking my car on red lines and in front of fire hydrants, just to test her assertion. She was right.

It was also because of 'Bama's new office that I learned that the West Virginia State Police had opened a file on me in Mineral County, which identified me for possible custodial detention if and when race riots started. Maura gave me the news late one night, whispering it over the phone. Old 'Bama, whom victory had made magnanimous, had wanted me to know and to be warned.

I remember feeling sick and scared . . . and then, when that passed, a little flattered. I was eighteen, had scarcely been outside Mineral County, and someone in authority decided I was dangerous? I mean, *I* liked to think so. But that an official establishment should collude with my fantasies of importance was quite another matter.

I took it as a sign that it was time for me to leave the Valley and go Elsewhere. I did leave it, that very fall, packing my bags for New Haven. But leaving it *behind* was never a possibility. It did not take me long to realize that.

The "Personal Statement" for my Yale application began: "My grandfather was colored, my father was Negro, and I am black." And it concluded: "As always, whitey now sits in judgment of me, preparing to cast my fate. It is your decision either to let me blow with the wind as a non-entity or to encourage the development of self. Allow me to prove myself."

I wince at the rhetoric today, but they let me in.

18 / Walk the Last Mile

Mama came to believe early on that the key to wealth and comfort in America was owning property. She wanted a nice house for the same reason she liked nice things. But she wanted to own a piece of *earth* too. Because colored people were hindered from owning property in Piedmont throughout the years of my childhood, our houses were always rented.

So Mama always wanted to buy a house. She was possessed by the subject. The funny thing, though, is that up to the very end, she would say that her first home with Daddy was her favorite. And now that I have been married for two decades, I understand how a house for four people that was as big as a postage stamp could be re-created by imagination and memory as a château. She loved it because she was happy, and in love, and in love with her life there. This would not always be so. But none of that stopped her from moving.

Unfortunately for Mama, the only person in the Gates family I ever heard of who didn't care for owning property was Daddy. Just Mama's luck, and ours. Daddy was terrified of debt. So even in the late sixties, when her brother Earkie established a precedent by purchasing the Coleman family house, he still wasn't interested. And the inability to own became one of Mama's great frustrations.

Where Daddy shied from debt, Mama was intrepid, at least until the change. She could leverage Daddy's two salaries like a Wall Street financier. But Miss Pauline wanted a house, and that was tantalizingly out of reach.

She started buying house books and magazines. Dozens, for research. She and I would look at them, just as I would study the pages of the three or four mail order catalogues we'd regularly receive: Ward's, Sears, Roebuck, General Merchandise, Mayer's. (Almost all of our Christmas gifts came from General Merchandise.)

At one point, Mama's plan was to build a house, on land near her mother or brothers on Erin Street. The first time I ever saw Mama *really* angry at my father—much angrier than when she'd accuse him of flirting with Miss Noll or Miss Mary—was on the day when he killed the deal that would have let us build a sort of family complex with two or three of Mama's brothers. We had the plans, the land was picked out (just below Big Mom's, near where Miss Lizzy's dogs barked at night when the Sneakin' Deacon made his rounds visiting his parishioners), and Mama was all excited. Radiant, in fact. She loved to dream, like all the Colemans, and she loved to make things *happen*, which was more Gates than Coleman. (When it came to finance and risk, Daddy was more Coleman than Gates.)

"We're not going to do it," Daddy said.

"Why not?" Mama demanded.

"Because I'm not going to sign the papers."

That was it. The whole thing. I don't think Mama ever got over it. Not until they bought the old Thomas house on East Hampshire Street, if then.

Mrs. Thomas was an old white lady for whom Mama had

worked when she was a little girl. I never met Mrs. Thomas, but I knew the name because Mama would mention her to Daddy once in a while. She and her husband had a son, Paul, who went off to college and became some sort of executive. He lived Elsewhere. "I used to call all colored women Dorothy," Paul told me later, "because Dorothy Coleman [Nemo's wife] was our maid, and I loved her so much."

I thought that was sweet. Racist cracker, Daddy would later say. Then he'd laugh: All niggers do *kinda* look alike.

Cut to 1960. I was all of ten years old and was sitting in the living room of Mrs. Thomas's house. She had just been buried, and her son was selling off their antiques. Mama knew the furniture, because she had cleaned it. She was very comfortable with Paul too. He treated her with a great deal of respect, even deference.

Mama had something on her mind, some goal in sight, and she was determined to achieve it. So we had bathed and put on our good clothes. She was dressed to kill.

I want those two bookcases, Paul, she said straightforwardly. And the desk in your room.

Paul hadn't wanted to sell that desk, I suspect. He looked sort of blankly at Mama.

They *are* a set, she said.

They stared at each other for a little bit, like two animals dancing for dominance.

Is twenty dollars too much? Paul finally asked. When Paul went to get the receipt book, Mama whispered that maybe we'd live in a nice house like this someday.

One case went for our reference books, the other went down to Aunt Marguerite's, and the desk went to me. Elmer Shaver—Daddy's boss at the telephone company—bought the house.

Owning furniture wasn't the same as owning a house, and as I grew up, I resolved to do something about it.

Our rented house had been plenty big enough, until Mama started collecting obsessively, canned food and bolts of cloth for a rainy day, as she'd said at first. You never know when you'll need these things, she'd said. One day next Tuesday, Daddy would mumble under his breath, by which he meant the twelfth of never. All of us, even Daddy, used to spend long hours praying that one day next Tuesday would come soon. She hoarded items like someone who was afraid of being poor again, and she was immune to reassurance. She had even taken to hiding her money in the drawer of her bureau.

I came home from college one summer and walked up the pavement. When Mama opened the door, I saw her as if for the first time: so old and tired and despondent. The years of having her hair done had damaged her hair so much that she was going bald. She'd taken to wearing a wig. I know I look bad, she said, wiping her forehead, where the sweat ran down from under her wig. I am just so tired.

Opportunely, Elmer Shaver had decided to retire and sell the Thomas house he'd bought when I was ten. Rocky, Daddy and I pooled all our resources, including a few scholarship checks, and the deal was done.

The purchase of the Thomas house wasn't all I arranged at that time. I also prepared to go to court and change my name from Louis Smith Gates, as my birth certificate reads, to that of my father. Mama had promised her best friend, unmarried Miss Smith, that she'd pass her name on to the second-born, since the first-born was named for his grandfathers, Paul Coleman and Edward Gates. I had hated that name, Smith, felt deprived of my birthright. Finally, I got around to telling my parents. Then, oddly, I found myself climbing Up the Hill to tell my grandmother. "Thank the Lord," Big Mom said. "That name never made sense to me anyhow." A few days later, I was on the witness stand, responding to Judge Cuppett's questions about why I sought to do this thing after all this time. Because I love my father and because it is my true name, I said, in the presence of Mama and Daddy and my soon-to-be wife, Sharon, and a bailiff. We all cried and cried together at that courthouse in Keyser.

Completing the purchase of the Thomas house from the Shavers proved a more delicate affair. A year later, just after the closing, Mama decided she didn't want to move in. She preferred *this* house or *that* house. Even the Campbell house next door, which needed a complete renovation. She wasn't going to leave Erin Street. She didn't have enough furniture. The house was too big. It was too dark. Who'd cut the grass? The neighbors were racists.

Mama, what's wrong with you? I pleaded. We'll lose all our money.

It was a pitched battle, but Mama finally moved. Sharon and I bought a dining room set at Macy's—on a charge account that was soon canceled for nonpayment—rented a U-Haul, and drove it from New York City to the Valley. Mama's brothers unpacked it and carried it in. Rocky and his wife, Paula, and their two girls drove down from New Jersey. And we had one hell of a feast. Roast beef and brown potatoes; "baked baked beans"; baked corn; kale, well-seasoned, cooked for hours with a big piece of fatback. Then I asked Mama, in the quiet of the celebration's aftermath, just what all the rigmarole about not moving was all about.

Skippy, you'll never know, she said.

Then, haltingly, she began to talk.

Mrs. Thomas used to make me sit out in the kitchen, at a little wooden table, and eat the scraps. She was a mean woman. She used to leave money around, to see if I would steal it. She made me work on Thanksgiving and Christmas. She treated me bad. . . . The thought of moving into this house . . . I wanted to burn this house down.

Her eyes were glassy; she lowered her head, placing two

fingers on the bridge of her nose. It was a gesture of resignation; she was angry that the memories still had that power.

Mama cried for a long time. And she almost *never* cried.
But it was Mama's house now. And she had it a decent while
before the onset of her final depression, when she would sit
for most of the day in her big reclining chair, talking about
death if she talked at all. I'll never know if we did the right
thing by buying her that house, or whether our insistence on
vindicating her was somehow misguided.

It was 1986 and I had been at an out-of-town conference,
when I got the news. I'll never forget that slow walk down the
corridor to the hotel door. From a distance, I could see the
pink message slips taped all over my door. It had to be death
or its imminence, I thought. It had to be Mama. Messages
from the dean, from the police, from the department, from
my wife, my father, from the hotel manager, from the police
again. CALL HOME.

She had been in the hospital for a checkup, and she seemed
to be doing fine. The white lady sharing the room with her
said she was talking one minute and slumped over the next.
They kept her alive on a machine.

She's up, she's down, she might not make it through the
night. She's a little better? She's worse? She won't . . . not
even through the night? I flew out to Pittsburgh, the nearest
airport, at dawn, then rented a car from there, weeping all
the way. Sharon and the kids drove from Ithaca.

At the hospital, Mama kept looking up at me, then at the
big blue-gray machine, trying to ask something with her eyes.
She'd be fully awake and conscious, then they'd have to jump-
start her heart again. She'd come back as if she'd just been
asleep, asking that same question again with her eyes. We'd
go, we'd come, over the course of the day, till my family

finally got there, at about nine that night. She'd waited to say
goodbye.

It was about midnight when we agreed not to shock her
heart anymore. Rocky, by now an oral surgeon, had assumed
charge. I had told her how much I loved her, and she had
smiled that deep-down smile, something to take with her on
the road.

Nemo and Mama are buried near each other, in the new,
highly esteemed, and otherwise white cemetery just outside
Keyser, behind the hill overlooking Mr. Bump's trailer park.
It probably bothers Mama to be looking down at Nemo every
day, unless she has forgiven him for not calling her to say goodbye when Big Mom was dying.

It's the kind of cemetery that seems fake to me, with all the
headstones bronze and flat, exactly the same size. We got the
"deluxe" model and jazzed it up as best we could. It's got a little
poem on it, and a bas-relief flower. Maybe it should have just
said "Miss Pauline," because everybody'd know who that was.

I hate that cemetery. Not because of the lack of aesthetic
appeal; not because it's integrated; but because what Nemo
called the Power isn't there. When you go up on Radical Hill,
up past where Sherry Lewis used to live, enter the gate, and
take the dusty road to the colored cemetery . . . now, that's
a *cemetery*. All the markers have different shapes, and the
graves are laid out whopper-jawed. Upkeep varies, so some
graves look pretty disheveled. Not Daddy Paul's, of course,
and not Big Mom's, either.

This is where the old souls come to hide, resting till the
Day of the Lord. Falling out over graves, like I once saw Mr.
Bootsie do when I was a boy, listening to Mama perform her
eulogy. Please, please—just one more look, don't take her
yet, just one more look, was all he said, shouting and whooping
and hollering and falling out all over his mother's grave.

You had a chance, in a colored funeral. You had a chance to work out your grief. You didn't have to be in a hurry with it, either. You could touch it, play with it, and talk to it, letting it work itself up in its own good time. Mama said she didn't want one of those tearjerkers, with crepe-hangers sitting in the mourners' pew and then crowding around her grave. She wanted a closed casket, ten minutes at the max, and don't let Nemo officiate. That was when she was younger. She'd pick out her dress and wig hat, the jewelry and the shoes, when she got old. By the time my mother died, at the worst of her dejection and alienation from herself, her family, the Colemans, seemed to me coolly distant, somewhat embarrassed by her eccentricities and depression. They were tired of her, it almost seemed, and she was tired of life. I think by the end she wanted to die. Nor did she believe in an afterlife. She just wanted release.

Instead of the modern Episcopal Milquetoast service we had for Mama, I passionately wish that her funeral had been like the one for Miss Minnie, or the one for Papa Charlie— or the one for Uncle Boke, which happened back when I was five. That was a nice one.

The sermon was long and loud, demanding that you break down. He's with the Lord today, walking in grandeur past brooks and fountains, hand in hand with his mother, Miss Lucy Clifford, and his kind old father, Mr. Samuel. I know you want him back, but the Lord had need of him up there. Maybe it was to sing the tenor parts of the spirituals, or maybe to tend the fires. Maybe to polish the silver up nice, or to keep the gold real shiny. I *know* you'll miss him; we'll miss him too. But we'll meet again soon at the Pearly Gates. On that Great Day of the Judgment, when we cross over, he'll be waiting there for us, welcoming us into the fold.

Oh, man, did those sermons feel *good*, sad-good, and hurting. And then they'd sing that killer song, people falling out all along.

When I'm gone the last mile of the way
I will rest at the close of the day,
And I know there are joys that await me
When I've gone the last mile of the day.

Then Mama had risen to read her piece, looking all good and sounding all fine.

At Mama's funeral, I wanted to fall out like that, too. I wanted that blue-black preacher who had substituted that time for Reverend Mon-roe and had blown his tired ass away. I wanted him to get up on that pulpit and preach the Sermon of the Dry Bones, like he'd done for Uncle Boke. People *still* dated things by that sermon: Hey . . . that was two years, three months, fourteen days, seven hours, and five minutes after Brother Blue Gums preached the Sermon of the Dry Bones.

I wanted the Heavenly Gospel Choir to sing a lot of long, sad songs, and I wanted people to fall out. I wanted the church to be *hot*, with the windows closed, those paper-colored funeral home fans spreading the steam rather than cooling things down. I wanted starched collars to wilt and straightened hair to kink up and "go back," I wanted the kitchens crinkling up in that heat, crackling loud and long, before our very eyes. I wanted the whole world to know my mama's death and her glory while alive. I wanted to cry and cry and cry, so I could tell her how sorry I was for not being a good enough son. I wanted her to know that I could have tried to do more, I could have tried to understand better, I could have come home more. I wanted her to know that I had tried, and that I loved her like life itself, and that I would miss her now that she was gone. I wanted to be sad in that dark, holy place, and I wanted that sadness to last.

19 / The Last
Mill Picnic

Some colored people claimed that they welcomed the change, that it was progress, that it was what we had been working for for so very long, our own version of the civil rights movement and Dr. King. But nobody really believed that, I don't think. For who in their right mind wanted to attend the mill picnic with the white people, when it meant shutting the colored one down?

Just like they did Howard High School, Nemo's son, Little Jim, had said. I was only surprised that he said it out loud.

Everybody worked *so* hard to integrate the thing in the mid-sixties, Aunt Marguerite mused, because that was what we were supposed to do then, what with Dr. King and everything. But by the time those crackers made us join them, she added, we didn't want to go.

I wish I could say that the community rebelled, that everybody refused to budge, that we joined hands in a circle and sang "We Shall Not, We Shall Not Be Moved," followed by "We Shall Overcome." But we didn't. In fact, people preferred not to acknowledge the approaching end, as if a miracle could happen and this whole nightmare would go away.

It was the last colored mill picnic. Like the roll called up yonder, everybody was there, even Caldonia and Old Man Mose. But Freddie Taylor had brought his 45s and was playing the best of rhythm and blues like nobody could believe. "What Becomes of the Brokenhearted?" was the favorite oldie of the day, because Piedmont was a Jimmy Ruffin town. Mellow, and sad. A coffee-colored feeling, with lots of cream. Jerry Butler's "Hey, Western Union Man" and Marvin Gaye's "I Heard It Through the Grapevine" were the most requested recent songs.

We had all come back for it, the diaspora reversing itself. There was a gentle hum or rumble that kept the same pitch all through the day, a lazy sort of pace as we walked back and forth along the arc of parked cars and just-mowed grass at Carskadon's Farm. Timothy grass and raspberry, black-eyed Susans big as saucers, thistle and dandelion, and everywhere sumac. The greensward was an allergist's nightmare, cow pies were a perpetual threat. Still, we walked.

They had tried to shut down Walden Methodist first, but Big Mom, the matriarch, had simply refused to stop attending her church of eight decades. And "the boys"—her sons, the Colemans—had of course supported her. Other than her doctor, Big Mom almost never saw white people. Nor did she care to be with or worship with them. People huddled together and lobbied her, then huddled together and lobbied her some more, to no avail. Big Mom wasn't going to stop attending Walden Methodist. And that was that. Since she had a weak heart and high blood pressure, had lost most of her sight because of a degenerating retina, couldn't hear unless you spoke in her ear—and had, above all else, a steely sense of resolve—*nobody* messed with Big Mom.

The white minister at the newly integrated United Methodist Church, over in the Orchard, would preach his normal sermon and then traipse over to Back Street and minister to

Big Mom, Mr. Ozzie, Mr. Doug Twyman, Mr. Lynn Allen, and a Coleman son or two. Miss Toot and her daughters, Frieda and Eudie, would still sing gospel, including "The Prodigal Son." White people can't preach too good, was all that Big Mom would volunteer about her experience with integration. I know she thought that God was white: there were all those pictures hanging on her walls. But that was another matter.

They might have kept Walden Methodist, but there was no hope for the mill pic-a-nic. And what was worse was that nobody had known what to do to reverse it. The mill administration itself made the decision, it said, because the law forbade separate but equal everything, including picnics. So the last wave of the civil rights era finally came to the Potomac Valley, crashing down upon the colored world of Piedmont. When it did, its most beloved, and cementing, ritual was doomed to give way. Nobody wanted segregation, you understand; but nobody thought of this as segregation.

So much was the way I remembered these occasions from my earliest childhood, and yet a new age had plainly dawned, an age that made the institution of a segregated picnic seem an anachronism. All of the people under thirty-five or so sported newly coiffed Afros, neatly rounded and shiny with Afro-Sheen. There were red and black and green dashikis everywhere, blousing over bell-bottomed trousers. Gold peace symbols dangled over leather vests, bare nigger toes poked out of fine leather sandals. Soul handshakes filled the air, as did the curious vocatives "brother" and "sister." I found myself looking for silk socks and stocking-cap waves, sleeveless see-through T-shirts peeking over the open neck of an unbuttoned silk shirt, Eye-talian style. Like Uncle Joe liked to wear when he dressed up. For bottles of whiskey and cheap wine in brown paper bags, furtively shared behind the open trunks of newly waxed cars, cleaned for the occasion, like Mr. Bootsie and Jingles and Mr. Roebuck Johnson used to do. Even the gamblers didn't have much to say, as they laid their cards down one by one, rather than slapping them down in the bid whist way, talking shit, talking trash, the way it used to be, the way it always was. The way it was supposed to be.

Miss Sarah Russell was there, carrying that black Bible with the reddish-orange pages—the one that printed the Sacred Name of Jesus and His words in bold red letters—still warning everybody about the end of the world and reminding us that Jesus wasn't going to be sending us a postcard or a telegram when He returned to judge us for our sins. He'd be coming like a thief in the night. The signs of the times are near, she shouted, the signs of the times. Don't nobody know the season but for the blooming of the trees. There's war and then there's the rumors of wars. My God is a harsh master, and the Holy Ghost has unloosed the fire of the spirit, and we know that fire by the talking in tongues.

Whenever Miss Sarah came around, Mr. Bootsie, Mr. Johnson, and Mr. Jingles would never drink out of whatever it was they kept in those brown paper bags. She appreciated that.

Mr. Bootsie and Mr. Marshall were running their card game at its usual place in the arc of parked automobiles, hoping that Miss Sarah would just keep walking by, as she made the rounds, fulfilling her obligation to remind her friends about Jesus' imminent return, and sharing a cool glass of lemonade and maybe a crisp fried chicken leg as she paused to catch her breath. Miss Ezelle had on a bright-red dress—she always *did* look good in red—and she was telling Mr. Buddy Green to lower his voice and not talk about how much money he was losing at poker until Miss Sarah got out of the way.

Greg and I, spying Miss Sarah over by the gamblers' card table, made a beeline down to the river, figuring that Jeannie and Tanya Hollingsworth had probably decided to go swimming by now. And Miss Sarah Russell, despite all the symbolism of water in the Bible, would never have been caught dead down by the river, where all that bare brown flesh, glistening in the sunshine, could prove too distracting even to the saved.

No one was at the river yet, so we headed back up the bank, passed Nemo's cast-iron vat, where he boiled the corn, and headed over to watch the last softball game, the game that pitted the alumni of Howard High School against the alumni of Everyplace Else. Roebuck Johnson was there, standing next to Mr. Comby Curl, the latter's wavy hair shining even more brightly than usual and sliced neatly by the part that he had shaved himself with that same straight-edged razor that made the back of my neck break out in shaving bumps. Involuntarily, I rubbed the back of my neck with my left hand, to see if they had disappeared yet. They were still there from yesterday's haircut. Roebuck was watching the game because he loved sports and also to escape the prying eye of all of his competing interests and loyalties. But it was exhilarating to watch the Howard team, headed by Earkie and Raymond, beat the hell out of the team from Elsewhere, just like they did every year. Only this time, the beating seemed more relentless. Poochie Taylor—who many people thought was the best natural athlete in a kingdom of natural athletes— tore the leather off the softball. "Couldn't stand to be away from the Valley," was what they said when he came home from spring training in the big leagues. Everybody had wanted him to make it to the World Series, just to beat the racist Yankees. Instead, he went to work up at the mill and then got his own church as a pastor. Everybody said he was sincere, unlike some of the other born-agains.

I was surprised that no one made any speeches, that no one commemorated the passing of the era in a formal way. But it did seem that people were walking back and forth through Carskadon's field a lot more times than they normally did, storing up memories to last until the day when somebody, somehow, would figure out a way to trick the paper mill into sponsoring this thing again. Maybe that's why Miss Ezelle seemed to take extra care to make her lips as red as Sammy Amoroso's strawberries in late August, and why Uncle Joe had used an extra dab of Brylcreem that morning, to give his silver DA that extra bit of shine. And why Miss Toot's high-pitched laughter could be heard all over that field all the day long, as she and Mr. Marshall beat all comers in a "rise and fly" marathon match of bid whist. So everyone could remember. We would miss the crackle of the brown paper bag in which Mr. Terry Conway hid his bottle of whiskey, and the way he'd wet his lips just before he'd tilt his whole body backwards and swig it down. The way he'd make the nastiest face after he drank it, as if he had tasted poison itself. When the bottle ran out, Mr. Terry would sleep himself back to health in the cool dawn splendor of a West Virginia morning.

Nor were there any fights at the colored Legion that night, not even after Inez Jones, with George Mason's white handkerchief dangling between her legs, did the dirty dog to end all dirty dogs.

The colored mill picnic would finish its run peaceably, then, if with an air of wistful resignation. All I know is that Nemo's corn never tasted saltier, his coffee never smelled fresher, than when these hundreds of Negroes gathered to say goodbye to themselves, their heritage, and their sole link to each other, wiped out of existence by the newly enforced anti–Jim Crow laws. The mill didn't want a lawsuit like the one brought against the Swordfish.

Yeah, even the Yankees had colored players now, Mr. Ozzie mumbled to Daddy, as they packed up Nemo's black cast-iron vat, hoping against hope to boil that corn another day.

ACKNOWLEDGMENTS

I would like to thank the Rockefeller Foundation for a fellowship that gave me a period of uninterrupted writing time at the Rockefeller Conference Center in Bellagio, where I began this book; the Center's staff for all their help, especially Pasquale Pesce, Gianna Celli, Elena Ongania, and Antonella Acanfora; and the Fellows for allowing me to read long sections of the manuscript on two occasions. Sharon Adams, Jennifer Bernstein, Kevin Bourke, Carl Brandt, Jamaica Kincaid, Nanci Kincaid, Sieglinde Lemke, Nader Alexander Mousavizadeh, and Ash Green all read the manuscript and were generous with their suggestions. I'm especially indebted to the astute editorial counsel of Henry Finder, Elizabeth Maguire, and LuAnn Walther. In addition, I would like to thank Sandra Leonard and Joanne Kendall for typing drafts of my manuscript. Finally, I would like to thank my family, friends, and the members of the Class of 1968 at Piedmont High School for their loving support all these years.

Henry Louis Gates, Jr., was born and raised in Mineral County, West Virginia. He graduated summa cum laude from Yale with a degree in history and was a London correspondent for *Time* magazine before receiving his Ph.D. in English from Cambridge University. He writes frequently for such publications as *Harper's*, *The New York Times Book Review*, *The New Yorker*, and the *Village Voice*; his books include *Figures in Black*, *The Signifying Monkey* (for which he received an American Book Award), and *Loose Canons*. He is now Professor of English and Chairman of Afro-American studies at Harvard University.

A NOTE ON THE TYPE

This book was set in a digitized version of Caledonia, designed
by W. A. Dwiggins (1880–1956). It belongs to the family of
printing types called "modern face" by printers—a term used
to mark the change in style of type letters that occurred about
1800. Caledonia borders on the general design of Scotch Ro-
man, but is more freely drawn that that letter.

Composed by Crane Typesetting Service, Inc.,
West Barnstable, Massachusetts
Printed and bound by The Haddon Craftsmen,
Scranton, Pennsylvania
Designed by Virginia Tan